Table of Contents

Articles of Agreement of the International Monetary Fund

Adopted at the United Nations Monetary and Financial Conference, Bretton Woods, New Hampshire, July 22, 1944. Entered into force December 27, 1945. Amended effective July 28, 1969, by the modifications approved by the Board of Governors in Resolution No. 23–5, adopted May 31, 1968; amended effective April 1, 1978, by the modifications approved by the Board of Governors in Resolution No. 31–4, adopted April 30, 1976; and amended effective November 11, 1992, by the modifications approved by the Board of Governors in Resolution No. 45–3, adopted June 28, 1990.

INTERNATIONAL MONETARY FUND
WASHINGTON, D.C.

International Standard Book Number: ISBN 1-55775-276-1

April 1993

Reprinted June 1998

Reprinted March 2000

Reprinted December 2004

Articles of agreement of the International Monetary Fund (1944).
Protocols, etc., 1992
Articles of agreements of the International Monetary Fund, adopted at the United Nations Monetary and Financial Conference, Bretton Woods, New Hampshire, July 22, 1994, entered into force December 27, 1945, amended effective July 28, 1969, by the modifications approved by the Board of Governors in Resolution No. 23–5. . . and amended effective November 11, 1992, by the modifications approved by the Board of Governors in Resolution No. 45–3, adopted June 28, 1990. — Washington. DC. : International Monetary Fund, 1992.
p. cm.

ISBN 1-55775-276-1

1. International Monetary Fund. I. Title: Articles of agreement of the International Monetary Fund. II. United Nations Monetary and Financial Conference (1944 : Bretton Woods, N.H.)
HG3881.5.I58A6 1992

SCHEDULES

ARTICLES OF AGREEMENT

Articles of Agreement of the International Monetary Fund

The Governments on whose behalf the present Agreement is signed agree as follows:

Introductory Article

(i) The International Monetary Fund is established and shall operate in accordance with the provisions of this Agreement as originally adopted and subsequently amended.

(ii) To enable the Fund to conduct its operations and transactions, the Fund shall maintain a General Department and a Special Drawing Rights Department. Membership in the Fund shall give the right to participation in the Special Drawing Rights Department.

(iii) Operations and transactions authorized by this Agreement shall be conducted through the General Department, consisting in accordance with the provisions of this Agreement of the General Resources Account, the Special Disbursement Account, and the Investment Account; except that operations and transactions involving special drawing rights shall be conducted through the Special Drawing Rights Department.

Article I

Purposes

The purposes of the International Monetary Fund are:

(i) To promote international monetary cooperation through a permanent institution which provides the machinery for consultation and collaboration on international monetary problems.

(ii) To facilitate the expansion and balanced growth of international trade, and to contribute thereby to the promotion and maintenance of high levels of employment and real income and to the development of the productive resources of all members as primary objectives of economic policy.

(iii) To promote exchange stability, to maintain orderly exchange arrangements among members, and to avoid competitive exchange depreciation.

(iv) To assist in the establishment of a multilateral system of payments in respect of current transactions between members and in the elimination of foreign exchange restrictions which hamper the growth of world trade.

(v) To give confidence to members by making the general resources of the Fund temporarily available to them under adequate safeguards, thus providing them with opportunity to correct maladjustments in their balance of payments without resorting to measures destructive of national or international prosperity.

(vi) In accordance with the above, to shorten the duration and lessen the degree of disequilibrium in the international balances of payments of members.

The Fund shall be guided in all its policies and decisions by the purposes set forth in this Article.

ARTICLE II

Membership

Section 1. *Original members*

The original members of the Fund shall be those of the countries represented at the United Nations Monetary and Financial Conference whose governments accept membership before December 31, 1945.

Section 2. *Other members*

Membership shall be open to other countries at such times and in accordance with such terms as may be prescribed by the Board of Governors. These terms, including the terms for subscriptions, shall be based on principles consistent with those applied to other countries that are already members.

ARTICLE III

Quotas and Subscriptions

Section 1. *Quotas and payment of subscriptions*

Each member shall be assigned a quota expressed in special drawing rights. The quotas of the members represented at the United Nations Monetary and Financial Conference which accept membership before December 31, 1945 shall be those set forth in Schedule A. The quotas of other members shall be determined by the Board of Governors. The subscription of each member shall be equal to its quota and shall be paid in full to the Fund at the appropriate depository.

Section 2. *Adjustment of quotas*

(*a*) The Board of Governors shall at intervals of not more than five years conduct a general review, and if it deems it appropriate propose an adjustment, of the quotas of the members. It may also, if it thinks fit, consider at any other time the adjustment of any particular quota at the request of the member concerned.

(*b*) The Fund may at any time propose an increase in the quotas of those members of the Fund that were members on August 31, 1975 in proportion to their quotas on that date in a cumulative amount not in excess of amounts transferred under Article V, Section 12(*f*)(i) and (*j*) from the Special Disbursement Account to the General Resources Account.

(*c*) An eighty-five percent majority of the total voting power shall be required for any change in quotas.

(*d*) The quota of a member shall not be changed until the member has consented and until payment has been made unless payment is deemed to have been made in accordance with Section 3(*b*) of this Article.

Section 3. *Payments when quotas are changed*

(*a*) Each member which consents to an increase in its quota under Section 2(*a*) of this Article shall, within a period determined by the Fund, pay to the Fund twenty-five percent of the increase in special drawing rights, but the Board of Governors may prescribe that this payment may be made, on the same basis for all members, in whole or in part in the currencies of other members specified, with their concurrence, by the Fund, or in the member's own currency. A non-participant shall pay in the currencies of other members specified by the Fund, with their concurrence, a proportion of the increase corresponding to the proportion to be paid in special drawing rights by participants. The balance of the increase shall be paid by the member in its own currency. The Fund's holdings of a member's currency shall not be increased above the level at which they would be subject to charges under Article V, Section 8(*b*)(ii), as a result of payments by other members under this provision.

(*b*) Each member which consents to an increase in its quota under Section 2(*b*) of this Article shall be deemed to have paid to the Fund an amount of subscription equal to such increase.

(*c*) If a member consents to a reduction in its quota, the Fund shall, within sixty days, pay to the member an amount equal to the reduction. The payment shall be made in the member's currency and in such amount of special drawing rights or the currencies of other members specified, with their concurrence, by the Fund as is necessary to prevent the reduction of the Fund's holdings of the currency below the new quota, provided that in exceptional circumstances the Fund may reduce its holdings of the currency below the new quota by payment to the member in its own currency.

(*d*) A seventy percent majority of the total voting power shall be required for any decision under (*a*) above, except for the determination of a period and the specification of currencies under that provision.

Section 4. *Substitution of securities for currency*

The Fund shall accept from any member, in place of any part of the member's currency in the General Resources Account which in the judgment of the Fund is not needed for its operations and transactions, notes or similar obligations issued by the member or the depository designated by the member under Article XIII, Section 2, which shall be non-negotiable, non-interest bearing and payable at their face value on demand by crediting the account of the Fund in the designated depository. This Section shall apply not only to currency subscribed by members but also to any currency otherwise due to, or acquired by, the Fund and to be placed in the General Resources Account.

ARTICLE IV

Obligations Regarding Exchange Arrangements

Section 1. *General obligations of members*

Recognizing that the essential purpose of the international monetary system is to provide a framework that facilitates the exchange of goods, services, and capital among countries, and that sustains sound economic growth, and that a principal objective is the continuing development of the orderly underlying conditions that are necessary for financial and economic stability, each member undertakes to collaborate with the Fund and other members to assure orderly exchange arrangements and to promote a stable system of exchange rates. In particular, each member shall:

(i) endeavor to direct its economic and financial policies toward the objective of fostering orderly economic growth with reasonable price stability, with due regard to its circumstances;

(ii) seek to promote stability by fostering orderly underlying economic and financial conditions and a monetary system that does not tend to produce erratic disruptions;

(iii) avoid manipulating exchange rates or the international monetary system in order to prevent effective balance of payments adjustment or to gain an unfair competitive advantage over other members; and

(iv) follow exchange policies compatible with the undertakings under this Section.

Section 2. *General exchange arrangements*

(*a*) Each member shall notify the Fund, within thirty days after the date of the second amendment of this Agreement, of the exchange arrangements it intends to apply in fulfillment of its obligations under Section 1 of this Article, and shall notify the Fund promptly of any changes in its exchange arrangements.

(*b*) Under an international monetary system of the kind prevailing on January 1, 1976, exchange arrangements may include (i) the maintenance by a member of a value for its currency in terms of the special drawing right or another denominator, other than gold, selected by the member, or (ii) cooperative arrangements by which members maintain the value of their currencies in relation to the value of the currency or currencies of other members, or (iii) other exchange arrangements of a member's choice.

(*c*) To accord with the development of the international monetary system, the Fund, by an eighty-five percent majority of the total voting power, may make provision for general exchange arrangements without limiting the right of members to have exchange arrangements of their choice consistent with the purposes of the Fund and the obligations under Section 1 of this Article.

Section 3. *Surveillance over exchange arrangements*

(*a*) The Fund shall oversee the international monetary system in order to ensure its effective operation, and shall oversee the compliance of each member with its obligations under Section 1 of this Article.

(*b*) In order to fulfill its functions under (*a*) above, the Fund shall exercise firm surveillance over the exchange rate policies of members, and shall adopt specific principles for the guidance of all members with respect to those policies. Each member shall provide the Fund with the information necessary for such surveillance, and, when requested by the Fund, shall consult with it on the member's exchange rate policies. The principles adopted by the Fund shall be consistent with cooperative arrangements by which members maintain the value of their currencies in relation to the value of the currency or currencies of other members, as well as with other exchange arrangements of a member's choice consistent with the purposes of the Fund and Section 1 of this Article. These principles shall respect the domestic social and political policies of members, and in applying these principles the Fund shall pay due regard to the circumstances of members.

Section 4. *Par values*

The Fund may determine, by an eighty-five percent majority of the total voting power, that international economic conditions permit the introduction of a widespread system of exchange arrangements based on stable but adjustable par values. The Fund shall make the determination on the basis of the underlying stability of the world economy, and for this purpose shall take into account price movements and rates of expansion in the economies of members. The determination shall be made in light of the evolution of the international monetary system, with particular reference to sources of liquidity, and, in order to ensure the effective operation of a system of par values, to arrangements under which both members in surplus and members in deficit in their balances of payments take prompt, effective, and symmetrical action to achieve adjustment, as well as to arrangements for intervention and the treatment of imbalances. Upon making such determination, the Fund shall notify members that the provisions of Schedule C apply.

Section 5. *Separate currencies within a member's territories*

(*a*) Action by a member with respect to its currency under this Article shall be deemed to apply to the separate currencies of all territories in respect of which the member has accepted this Agreement under Article XXXI, Section 2(*g*) unless the member declares that its action relates either to the metropolitan currency alone, or only to one or more specified separate currencies, or to the metropolitan currency and one or more specified separate currencies.

(*b*) Action by the Fund under this Article shall be deemed to relate to all currencies of a member referred to in (*a*) above unless the Fund declares otherwise.

Article V

Operations and Transactions of the Fund

Section 1. *Agencies dealing with the Fund*

Each member shall deal with the Fund only through its Treasury, central bank, stabilization fund, or other similar fiscal agency, and the Fund shall deal only with or through the same agencies.

Section 2. *Limitation on the Fund's operations and transactions*

(*a*) Except as otherwise provided in this Agreement, transactions on the account of the Fund shall be limited to transactions for the purpose of supplying a member, on the initiative of such member, with special drawing rights or the currencies of other members from the general resources of the Fund, which shall be held in the General Resources Account, in exchange for the currency of the member desiring to make the purchase.

(*b*) If requested, the Fund may decide to perform financial and technical services, including the administration of resources contributed by members, that are consistent with the purposes of the Fund. Operations involved in the performance of such financial services shall not be on the account of the Fund. Services under this subsection shall not impose any obligation on a member without its consent.

Section 3. *Conditions governing use of the Fund's general resources*

(*a*) The Fund shall adopt policies on the use of its general resources, including policies on stand-by or similar arrangements, and may adopt special policies for special balance of payments problems, that will assist members to solve their balance of payments problems in a manner consistent with the provisions of this Agreement and that will establish adequate safeguards for the temporary use of the general resources of the Fund.

(*b*) A member shall be entitled to purchase the currencies of other members from the Fund in exchange for an equivalent amount of its own currency subject to the following conditions:

(i) the member's use of the general resources of the Fund would be in accordance with the provisions of this Agreement and the policies adopted under them;

(ii) the member represents that it has a need to make the purchase because of its balance of payments or its reserve position or developments in its reserves;

(iii) the proposed purchase would be a reserve tranche purchase, or would not cause the Fund's holdings of the purchasing member's currency to exceed two hundred percent of its quota;

(iv) the Fund has not previously declared under Section 5 of this Article, Article VI, Section 1, or Article XXVI, Section 2(*a*) that the member desiring to purchase is ineligible to use the general resources of the Fund.

(*c*) The Fund shall examine a request for a purchase to determine whether the proposed purchase would be consistent with the provisions of this Agreement and the policies adopted under them, provided that requests for reserve tranche purchases shall not be subject to challenge.

(*d*) The Fund shall adopt policies and procedures on the selection of currencies to be sold that take into account, in consultation with members, the balance of payments and reserve position of members and developments in the exchange markets, as well as the desirability of promoting over time balanced positions in the Fund, provided that if a member represents that it is proposing to purchase the currency of another member because the purchasing member wishes to obtain an equivalent amount of its own currency offered by the other member, it shall be entitled to purchase the currency of the other member unless the Fund has given notice under Article VII, Section 3 that its holdings of the currency have become scarce.

(*e*) (i) Each member shall ensure that balances of its currency purchased from the Fund are balances of a freely usable currency or can be exchanged at the time of purchase for a freely usable currency of its choice at an exchange rate between the two currencies equivalent to the exchange rate between them on the basis of Article XIX, Section 7(*a*).

(ii) Each member whose currency is purchased from the Fund or is obtained in exchange for currency purchased from the Fund shall collaborate with the Fund and other members to enable such balances of its currency to be exchanged, at the time of purchase, for the freely usable currencies of other members.

(iii) An exchange under (i) above of a currency that is not freely usable shall be made by the member whose currency is purchased unless that member and the purchasing member agree on another procedure.

(iv) A member purchasing from the Fund the freely usable currency of another member and wishing to exchange it at the time of purchase for another freely usable currency shall make the exchange with the other member if requested by that member. The exchange shall be made for a freely usable currency selected by the other member at the rate of exchange referred to in (i) above.

(*f*) Under policies and procedures which it shall adopt, the Fund may agree to provide a participant making a purchase in accordance with this Section with special drawing rights instead of the currencies of other members.

Section 4. *Waiver of conditions*

The Fund may in its discretion, and on terms which safeguard its interests, waive any of the conditions prescribed in Section 3(*b*)(iii) and (iv) of this Article, especially in the case of members with a record of avoiding large or continuous use of the Fund's general resources. In making a waiver it shall take into consideration periodic or exceptional requirements of the member requesting the waiver. The Fund shall also take into consideration a member's willingness to pledge as collateral security acceptable assets having a value sufficient in the opinion of the Fund to protect its interests and may require as a condition of waiver the pledge of such collateral security.

Section 5. *Ineligibility to use the Fund's general resources*

Whenever the Fund is of the opinion that any member is using the general resources of the Fund in a manner contrary to the purposes of the Fund, it shall present to the member a report setting forth the views of the Fund and prescribing a suitable time for reply. After presenting such a report to a member, the Fund may limit the use of its general resources by the member. If no reply to the report is received from the member within the prescribed time, or if the reply received is unsatisfactory, the Fund may continue to limit the member's use of the general resources of the Fund or may, after giving reasonable notice to the member, declare it ineligible to use the general resources of the Fund.

Section 6. *Other purchases and sales of special drawing rights by the Fund*

(*a*) The Fund may accept special drawing rights offered by a participant in exchange for an equivalent amount of the currencies of other members.

(*b*) The Fund may provide a participant, at its request, with special drawing rights for an equivalent amount of the currencies of other members. The Fund's holdings of a member's currency shall not be increased as a result of these transactions above the level at which the holdings would be subject to charges under Section 8(*b*)(ii) of this Article.

(*c*) The currencies provided or accepted by the Fund under this Section shall be selected in accordance with policies that take into account the principles of Section 3(*d*) or 7(*i*) of this Article. The Fund may enter into transactions under this Section only if a member whose currency is provided or accepted by the Fund concurs in that use of its currency.

Section 7. *Repurchase by a member of its currency held by the Fund*

(*a*) A member shall be entitled to repurchase at any time the Fund's holdings of its currency that are subject to charges under Section 8(*b*) of this Article.

(*b*) A member that has made a purchase under Section 3 of this Article will be expected normally, as its balance of payments and reserve position improves, to repurchase the Fund's holdings of its currency that result from the purchase and are subject to charges under Section 8(*b*) of this Article. A member shall repurchase these holdings if, in accordance with policies on repurchase that the Fund shall adopt and after consultation with the member, the Fund represents to the member that it should repurchase because of an improvement in its balance of payments and reserve position.

(*c*) A member that has made a purchase under Section 3 of this Article shall repurchase the Fund's holdings of its currency that result from the purchase and are subject to charges under Section 8(*b*) of this Article not later than five years after the date on which the purchase was made. The Fund may prescribe that repurchase shall be made by a member in installments during the period beginning three years and ending five years after the date of a purchase. The Fund, by an eighty-five percent majority of the total voting power, may change the periods for repurchase under this subsection, and any period so adopted shall apply to all members.

(*d*) The Fund, by an eighty-five percent majority of the total voting power, may adopt periods other than those that apply in accordance with (*c*) above, which shall be the same for all members, for the repurchase of holdings of currency acquired by the Fund pursuant to a special policy on the use of its general resources.

(*e*) A member shall repurchase, in accordance with policies that the Fund shall adopt by a seventy percent majority of the total voting power, the Fund's holdings of its currency that are not acquired as a result of purchases and are subject to charges under Section 8(*b*)(ii) of this Article.

(*f*) A decision prescribing that under a policy on the use of the general resources of the Fund the period for repurchase under (*c*) or (*d*) above shall be shorter than the one in effect under the policy shall apply only to holdings acquired by the Fund subsequent to the effective date of the decision.

(*g*) The Fund, on the request of a member, may postpone the date of discharge of a repurchase obligation, but not beyond the maximum period under (*c*) or (*d*) above or under policies adopted by the Fund under (*e*) above, unless the Fund determines, by a seventy percent majority of the total voting power, that a longer period for repurchase which is consistent with the temporary use of the general resources of the Fund is justified because discharge on the due date would result in exceptional hardship for the member.

(*h*) The Fund's policies under Section 3(*d*) of this Article may be supplemented by policies under which the Fund may decide after consultation with a member to sell under Section 3(*b*) of this Article its holdings of the member's currency that have not been repurchased in accordance with this Section 7, without prejudice to any action that the Fund may be authorized to take under any other provision of this Agreement.

(*i*) All repurchases under this Section shall be made with special drawing rights or with the currencies of other members specified by the Fund. The Fund shall adopt policies and procedures with regard to the currencies to be used by members in making repurchases that take into account the principles in Section 3(*d*) of this Article. The Fund's holdings of a member's currency that is used in repurchase shall not be increased by the repurchase above the level at which they would be subject to charges under Section 8(*b*)(ii) of this Article.

(*j*) (i) If a member's currency specified by the Fund under (*i*) above is not a freely usable currency, the member shall ensure that the repurchasing member can obtain it at the time of the repurchase in exchange for a freely usable currency selected by the member whose currency has been specified. An exchange of currency under this provision shall take place at an exchange rate between the two currencies equivalent to the exchange rate between them on the basis of Article XIX, Section 7(*a*).

(ii) Each member whose currency is specified by the Fund for repurchase shall collaborate with the Fund and other members to enable repurchasing members, at the time of the repurchase, to obtain the specified currency in exchange for the freely usable currencies of other members.

(iii) An exchange under (*j*)(i) above shall be made with the member whose currency is specified unless that member and the repurchasing member agree on another procedure.

(iv) If a repurchasing member wishes to obtain, at the time of the repurchase, the freely usable currency of another member specified by the Fund under (*i*) above, it shall, if requested by the other member, obtain the currency from the other member in exchange for a freely usable currency at the rate of exchange referred to in (*j*)(i) above. The Fund may adopt regulations on the freely usable currency to be provided in an exchange.

Section 8. *Charges*

(*a*) (i) The Fund shall levy a service charge on the purchase by a member of special drawing rights or the currency of another member held in the General Resources Account in exchange for its own currency, provided that the Fund may levy a lower service charge on reserve tranche purchases than on other purchases. The service charge on reserve tranche purchases shall not exceed one-half of one percent.

(ii) The Fund may levy a charge for stand-by or similar arrangements. The Fund may decide that the charge for an arrangement shall be offset against the service charge levied under (i) above on purchases under the arrangement.

(*b*) The Fund shall levy charges on its average daily balances of a member's currency held in the General Resources Account to the extent that they

(i) have been acquired under a policy that has been the subject of an exclusion under Article XXX(*c*), or

(ii) exceed the amount of the member's quota after excluding any balances referred to in (i) above.

The rates of charge normally shall rise at intervals during the period in which the balances are held.

(*c*) If a member fails to make a repurchase required under Section 7 of this Article, the Fund, after consultation with the member on the reduction of the Fund's holdings of its currency, may impose such charges as the Fund deems appropriate on its holdings of the member's currency that should have been repurchased.

(*d*) A seventy percent majority of the total voting power shall be required for the determination of the rates of charge under (*a*) and (*b*) above, which shall be uniform for all members, and under (*c*) above.

(*e*) A member shall pay all charges in special drawing rights, provided that in exceptional circumstances the Fund may permit a member to pay charges in the currencies of other members specified by the Fund, after consultation with them, or in its own currency. The Fund's holdings of a member's currency shall not be increased as a result of payments by other members under this provision above the level at which they would be subject to charges under (*b*)(ii) above.

Section 9. *Remuneration*

(*a*) The Fund shall pay remuneration on the amount by which the percentage of quota prescribed under (*b*) or (*c*) below exceeds the Fund's average daily balances of a member's currency held in the General Resources Account other than balances acquired under a policy that has been the subject of an exclusion under Article XXX(*c*). The rate of remuneration, which shall be determined by the Fund by a seventy percent majority of the total voting power, shall be the same for all members and shall be not more than, nor less than four-fifths of, the rate of interest under Article XX, Section 3. In establishing the rate of remuneration, the Fund shall take into account the rates of charge under Article V, Section 8(*b*).

(b) The percentage of quota applying for the purposes of *(a)* above shall be:

(i) for each member that became a member before the second amendment of this Agreement, a percentage of quota corresponding to seventy-five percent of its quota on the date of the second amendment of this Agreement, and for each member that became a member after the date of the second amendment of this Agreement, a percentage of quota calculated by dividing the total of the amounts corresponding to the percentages of quota that apply to the other members on the date on which the member became a member by the total of the quotas of the other members on the same date; plus

(ii) the amounts it has paid to the Fund in currency or special drawing rights under Article III, Section 3(*a*) since the date applicable under (*b*)(i) above; and minus

(iii) the amounts it has received from the Fund in currency or special drawing rights under Article III, Section 3(*c*) since the date applicable under (*b*)(i) above.

(*c*) The Fund, by a seventy percent majority of the total voting power, may raise the latest percentage of quota applying for the purposes of (*a*) above to each member to:

(i) a percentage, not in excess of one hundred percent, that shall be determined for each member on the basis of the same criteria for all members, or

(ii) one hundred percent for all members.

(*d*) Remuneration shall be paid in special drawing rights, provided that either the Fund or the member may decide that the payment to the member shall be made in its own currency.

Section 10. *Computations*

(*a*) The value of the Fund's assets held in the accounts of the General Department shall be expressed in terms of the special drawing right.

(*b*) All computations relating to currencies of members for the purpose of applying the provisions of this Agreement, except Article IV and Schedule C, shall be at the rates at which the Fund accounts for these currencies in accordance with Section 11 of this Article.

(*c*) Computations for the determination of amounts of currency in relation to quota for the purpose of applying the provisions of this Agreement shall not include currency held in the Special Disbursement Account or in the Investment Account.

Section 11. *Maintenance of value*

(*a*) The value of the currencies of members held in the General Resources Account shall be maintained in terms of the special drawing right in accordance with exchange rates under Article XIX, Section 7(*a*).

(*b*) An adjustment in the Fund's holdings of a member's currency pursuant to this Section shall be made on the occasion of the use of that currency in an operation or transaction between the Fund and another member and at such other times as the Fund may decide or the member may request. Payments to or by the Fund in respect of an adjustment shall be made within a reasonable time, as determined by the Fund, after the date of adjustment, and at any other time requested by the member.

Section 12. *Other operations and transactions*

(*a*) The Fund shall be guided in all its policies and decisions under this Section by the objectives set forth in Article VIII, Section 7 and by the objective of avoiding the management of the price, or the establishment of a fixed price, in the gold market.

(*b*) Decisions of the Fund to engage in operations or transactions under (*c*), (*d*), and (*e*) below shall be made by an eighty-five percent majority of the total voting power.

(*c*) The Fund may sell gold for the currency of any member after consulting the member for whose currency the gold is sold, provided that the Fund's holdings of a member's currency held in the General Resources Account shall not be increased by the sale above the level at which they would be subject to charges under Section 8(*b*)(ii) of this Article without the concurrence of the member, and provided that, at the request of the member, the Fund at the time of sale shall exchange for the currency of another member such part of the currency received as would prevent such an increase. The exchange of a currency for the currency of another member shall be made after consultation with that member, and shall not increase the Fund's holdings of that member's currency above the level at which they would be subject to charges under Section 8(*b*)(ii) of this Article. The Fund shall adopt policies and procedures with regard to exchanges that take into account the principles applied under Section 7(*i*) of this Article. Sales under this provision to a member shall be at a price agreed for each transaction on the basis of prices in the market.

(*d*) The Fund may accept payments from a member in gold instead of special drawing rights or currency in any operations or transactions under this Agreement. Payments to the Fund under this provision shall be at a price agreed for each operation or transaction on the basis of prices in the market.

(*e*) The Fund may sell gold held by it on the date of the second amendment of this Agreement to those members that were members on August 31, 1975 and that agree to buy it, in proportion to their quotas on that date. If the Fund intends to sell gold under (*c*) above for the purpose of (*f*)(ii) below, it may sell to each developing member that agrees to buy it that portion of the gold which, if sold under (*c*) above, would have produced the excess that could have been distributed to it under (*f*)(iii) below. The gold that would be sold under this provision to a member that has been declared ineligible to use the general resources of the Fund under Section 5 of this Article shall be sold to it when the ineligibility ceases, unless the Fund decides to make the sale sooner. The sale of gold to a member under this subsection (*e*) shall be made in exchange for its currency and at a price equivalent at the time of sale to one special drawing right per 0.888 671 gram of fine gold.

(*f*) Whenever under (*c*) above the Fund sells gold held by it on the date of the second amendment of this Agreement, an amount of the proceeds equivalent at the time of sale to one special drawing right per 0.888 671 gram of fine gold shall be placed in the General Resources Account and, except as the Fund may decide otherwise under (*g*) below, any excess shall be held in the Special Disbursement Account. The assets held in the Special Disbursement Account shall be held separately from the other accounts of the General Department, and may be used at any time:

(i) to make transfers to the General Resources Account for immediate use in operations and transactions authorized by provisions of this Agreement other than this Section;

(ii) for operations and transactions that are not authorized by other provisions of this Agreement but are consistent with the purposes of the Fund. Under this subsection (*f*)(ii) balance of payments assistance may be made available on special terms to developing members in difficult circumstances, and for this purpose the Fund shall take into account the level of per capita income;

(iii) for distribution to those developing members that were members on August 31, 1975, in proportion to their quotas on that date, of such part of the assets that the Fund decides to use for the purposes of (ii) above as corresponds to the proportion of the quotas of these members on the date of distribution to the total of the quotas of all members on the same date, provided that the distribution under this provision to a member that has been declared ineligible to use the general resources of the Fund under Section 5 of this Article shall be made when the ineligibility ceases, unless the Fund decides to make the distribution sooner.

Decisions to use assets pursuant to (i) above shall be taken by a seventy percent majority of the total voting power, and decisions pursuant to (ii) and (iii) above shall be taken by an eighty-five percent majority of the total voting power.

(*g*) The Fund may decide, by an eighty-five percent majority of the total voting power, to transfer a part of the excess referred to in (*f*) above to the Investment Account for use pursuant to the provisions of Article XII, Section 6(*f*).

(*h*) Pending uses specified under (*f*) above, the Fund may invest a member's currency held in the Special Disbursement Account in marketable obligations of that member or in marketable obligations of international financial organizations. The income of investment and interest received under (*f*)(ii) above shall be placed in the Special Disbursement Account. No investment shall be made without the concurrence of the member whose currency is used to make the investment. The Fund shall invest only in obligations denominated in special drawing rights or in the currency used for investment.

(*i*) The General Resources Account shall be reimbursed from time to time in respect of the expenses of administration of the Special Disbursement Account paid from the General Resources Account by transfers from the Special Disbursement Account on the basis of a reasonable estimate of such expenses.

(*j*) The Special Disbursement Account shall be terminated in the event of the liquidation of the Fund and may be terminated prior to liquidation of the Fund by a seventy percent majority of the total voting power. Upon termination of the account because of the liquidation of the Fund, any assets in this account shall be distributed in accordance with the provisions of Schedule K. Upon termination prior to liquidation of the Fund, any assets in this account shall be transferred to the General Resources Account for immediate use in operations and transactions. The Fund, by a seventy percent majority of the total voting power, shall adopt rules and regulations for the administration of the Special Disbursement Account.

Article VI

Capital Transfers

Section 1. *Use of the Fund's general resources for capital transfers*

(*a*) A member may not use the Fund's general resources to meet a large or sustained outflow of capital except as provided in Section 2 of this Article, and the Fund may request a member to exercise controls to prevent such use of the general resources of the Fund. If, after receiving such a request, a member fails to exercise appropriate controls, the Fund may declare the member ineligible to use the general resources of the Fund.

(*b*) Nothing in this Section shall be deemed:

(i) to prevent the use of the general resources of the Fund for capital transactions of reasonable amount required for the expansion of exports or in the ordinary course of trade, banking, or other business; or

(ii) to affect capital movements which are met out of a member's own resources, but members undertake that such capital movements will be in accordance with the purposes of the Fund.

Section 2. *Special provisions for capital transfers*

A member shall be entitled to make reserve tranche purchases to meet capital transfers.

Section 3. *Controls of capital transfers*

Members may exercise such controls as are necessary to regulate international capital movements, but no member may exercise these controls in a manner which will restrict payments for current transactions or which will unduly delay transfers of funds in settlement of commitments, except as provided in Article VII, Section 3(*b*) and in Article XIV, Section 2.

Article VII

Replenishment and Scarce Currencies

Section 1. *Measures to replenish the Fund's holdings of currencies*

The Fund may, if it deems such action appropriate to replenish its holdings of any member's currency in the General Resources

Account needed in connection with its transactions, take either or both of the following steps:

(i) propose to the member that, on terms and conditions agreed between the Fund and the member, the latter lend its currency to the Fund or that, with the concurrence of the member, the Fund borrow such currency from some other source either within or outside the territories of the member, but no member shall be under any obligation to make such loans to the Fund or to concur in the borrowing of its currency by the Fund from any other source;

(ii) require the member, if it is a participant, to sell its currency to the Fund for special drawing rights held in the General Resources Account, subject to Article XIX, Section 4. In replenishing with special drawing rights, the Fund shall pay due regard to the principles of designation under Article XIX, Section 5.

Section 2. *General scarcity of currency*

If the Fund finds that a general scarcity of a particular currency is developing, the Fund may so inform members and may issue a report setting forth the causes of the scarcity and containing recommendations designed to bring it to an end. A representative of the member whose currency is involved shall participate in the preparation of the report.

Section 3. *Scarcity of the Fund's holdings*

(*a*) If it becomes evident to the Fund that the demand for a member's currency seriously threatens the Fund's ability to supply that currency, the Fund, whether or not it has issued a report under Section 2 of this Article, shall formally declare such currency scarce and shall thenceforth apportion its existing and accruing supply of the scarce currency with due regard to the relative needs of members, the general international economic situation, and any other pertinent considerations. The Fund shall also issue a report concerning its action.

(*b*) A formal declaration under (*a*) above shall operate as an authorization to any member, after consultation with the Fund, temporarily to impose limitations on the freedom of exchange operations in the scarce currency. Subject to the provisions of Article IV and

Schedule C, the member shall have complete jurisdiction in determining the nature of such limitations, but they shall be no more restrictive than is necessary to limit the demand for the scarce currency to the supply held by, or accruing to, the member in question, and they shall be relaxed and removed as rapidly as conditions permit.

(*c*) The authorization under (*b*) above shall expire whenever the Fund formally declares the currency in question to be no longer scarce.

Section 4. *Administration of restrictions*

Any member imposing restrictions in respect of the currency of any other member pursuant to the provisions of Section 3(*b*) of this Article shall give sympathetic consideration to any representations by the other member regarding the administration of such restrictions.

Section 5. *Effect of other international agreements on restrictions*

Members agree not to invoke the obligations of any engagements entered into with other members prior to this Agreement in such manner as will prevent the operation of the provisions of this Article.

Article VIII

General Obligations of Members

Section 1. *Introduction*

In addition to the obligations assumed under other articles of this Agreement, each member undertakes the obligations set out in this Article.

Section 2. *Avoidance of restrictions on current payments*

(*a*) Subject to the provisions of Article VII, Section 3(*b*) and Article XIV, Section 2, no member shall, without the approval of the Fund, impose restrictions on the making of payments and transfers for current international transactions.

(*b*) Exchange contracts which involve the currency of any member and which are contrary to the exchange control regulations of that member maintained or imposed consistently with this Agreement shall be unenforceable in the territories of any member. In addition, members may, by mutual accord, cooperate in measures for the purpose of making the exchange control regulations of either member more effective, provided that such measures and regulations are consistent with this Agreement.

Section 3. *Avoidance of discriminatory currency practices*

No member shall engage in, or permit any of its fiscal agencies referred to in Article V, Section 1 to engage in, any discriminatory currency arrangements or multiple currency practices, whether within or outside margins under Article IV or prescribed by or under Schedule C, except as authorized under this Agreement or approved by the Fund. If such arrangements and practices are engaged in at the date when this Agreement enters into force, the member concerned shall consult with the Fund as to their progressive removal unless they are maintained or imposed under Article XIV, Section 2, in which case the provisions of Section 3 of that Article shall apply.

Section 4. *Convertibility of foreign-held balances*

(*a*) Each member shall buy balances of its currency held by another member if the latter, in requesting the purchase, represents:

(i) that the balances to be bought have been recently acquired as a result of current transactions; or

(ii) that their conversion is needed for making payments for current transactions.

The buying member shall have the option to pay either in special drawing rights, subject to Article XIX, Section 4, or in the currency of the member making the request.

(*b*) The obligation in (*a*) above shall not apply when:

(i) the convertibility of the balances has been restricted consistently with Section 2 of this Article or Article VI, Section 3;

(ii) the balances have accumulated as a result of transactions effected before the removal by a member of restrictions maintained or imposed under Article XIV, Section 2;

(iii) the balances have been acquired contrary to the exchange regulations of the member which is asked to buy them;

(iv) the currency of the member requesting the purchase has been declared scarce under Article VII, Section 3(*a*); or

(v) the member requested to make the purchase is for any reason not entitled to buy currencies of other members from the Fund for its own currency.

Section 5. *Furnishing of information*

(*a*) The Fund may require members to furnish it with such information as it deems necessary for its activities, including, as the minimum necessary for the effective discharge of the Fund's duties, national data on the following matters:

(i) official holdings at home and abroad of (1) gold, (2) foreign exchange;

(ii) holdings at home and abroad by banking and financial agencies, other than official agencies, of (1) gold, (2) foreign exchange;

(iii) production of gold;

(iv) gold exports and imports according to countries of destination and origin;

(v) total exports and imports of merchandise, in terms of local currency values, according to countries of destination and origin;

(vi) international balance of payments, including (1) trade in goods and services, (2) gold transactions, (3) known capital transactions, and (4) other items;

(vii) international investment position, i.e., investments within the territories of the member owned abroad and investments abroad owned by persons in its territories so far as it is possible to furnish this information;

(viii) national income;

(ix) price indices, i.e., indices of commodity prices in wholesale and retail markets and of export and import prices;

(x) buying and selling rates for foreign currencies;

(xi) exchange controls, i.e., a comprehensive statement of exchange controls in effect at the time of assuming membership in the Fund and details of subsequent changes as they occur; and

(xii) where official clearing arrangements exist, details of amounts awaiting clearance in respect of commercial and financial transactions, and of the length of time during which such arrears have been outstanding.

(*b*) In requesting information the Fund shall take into consideration the varying ability of members to furnish the data requested. Members shall be under no obligation to furnish information in such detail that the affairs of individuals or corporations are disclosed. Members undertake, however, to furnish the desired information in as detailed and accurate a manner as is practicable and, so far as possible, to avoid mere estimates.

(*c*) The Fund may arrange to obtain further information by agreement with members. It shall act as a centre for the collection and exchange of information on monetary and financial problems, thus facilitating the preparation of studies designed to assist members in developing policies which further the purposes of the Fund.

Section 6. *Consultation between members regarding existing international agreements*

Where under this Agreement a member is authorized in the special or temporary circumstances specified in the Agreement to maintain or establish restrictions on exchange transactions, and there are other engagements between members entered into prior to this Agreement which conflict with the application of such restrictions, the parties to such engagements shall consult with one another with a view to making such mutually acceptable adjustments as may be necessary. The provisions of this Article shall be without prejudice to the operation of Article VII, Section 5.

Section 7. *Obligation to collaborate regarding policies on reserve assets*

Each member undertakes to collaborate with the Fund and with other members in order to ensure that the policies of the member with respect to reserve assets shall be consistent with the objectives of promoting better international surveillance of international liquidity and making the special drawing right the principal reserve asset in the international monetary system.

Article IX

Status, Immunities, and Privileges

Section 1. *Purposes of Article*

To enable the Fund to fulfill the functions with which it is entrusted, the status, immunities, and privileges set forth in this Article shall be accorded to the Fund in the territories of each member.

Section 2. *Status of the Fund*

The Fund shall possess full juridical personality, and in particular, the capacity:

(i) to contract;

(ii) to acquire and dispose of immovable and movable property; and

(iii) to institute legal proceedings.

Section 3. *Immunity from judicial process*

The Fund, its property and its assets, wherever located and by whomsoever held, shall enjoy immunity from every form of judicial process except to the extent that it expressly waives its immunity for the purpose of any proceedings or by the terms of any contract.

Section 4. *Immunity from other action*

Property and assets of the Fund, wherever located and by whomsoever held, shall be immune from search, requisition, confiscation, expropriation, or any other form of seizure by executive or legislative action.

Section 5. *Immunity of archives*

The archives of the Fund shall be inviolable.

Section 6. *Freedom of assets from restrictions*

To the extent necessary to carry out the activities provided for in this Agreement, all property and assets of the Fund shall be free from restrictions, regulations, controls, and moratoria of any nature.

Section 7. *Privilege for communications*

The official communications of the Fund shall be accorded by members the same treatment as the official communications of other members.

Section 8. *Immunities and privileges of officers and employees*

All Governors, Executive Directors, Alternates, members of committees, representatives appointed under Article XII, Section 3(*j*), advisors of any of the foregoing persons, officers, and employees of the Fund:

(i) shall be immune from legal process with respect to acts performed by them in their official capacity except when the Fund waives this immunity;

(ii) not being local nationals, shall be granted the same immunities from immigration restrictions, alien registration requirements, and national service obligations and the same facilities as regards exchange restrictions as are accorded by members to the representatives, officials, and employees of comparable rank of other members; and

(iii) shall be granted the same treatment in respect of traveling facilities as is accorded by members to representatives, officials, and employees of comparable rank of other members.

Section 9. *Immunities from taxation*

(*a*) The Fund, its assets, property, income, and its operations and transactions authorized by this Agreement shall be immune from all taxation and from all customs duties. The Fund shall also be immune from liability for the collection or payment of any tax or duty.

(*b*) No tax shall be levied on or in respect of salaries and emoluments paid by the Fund to Executive Directors, Alternates, officers, or employees of the Fund who are not local citizens, local subjects, or other local nationals.

(*c*) No taxation of any kind shall be levied on any obligation or security issued by the Fund, including any dividend or interest thereon, by whomsoever held:

(i) which discriminates against such obligation or security solely because of its origin; or

(ii) if the sole jurisdictional basis for such taxation is the place or currency in which it is issued, made payable or paid, or the location of any office or place of business maintained by the Fund.

Section 10. *Application of Article*

Each member shall take such action as is necessary in its own territories for the purpose of making effective in terms of its own law the principles set forth in this Article and shall inform the Fund of the detailed action which it has taken.

ARTICLE X

Relations with Other International Organizations

The Fund shall cooperate within the terms of this Agreement with any general international organization and with public international organizations having specialized responsibilities in related fields. Any arrangements for such cooperation which would involve a modification of any provision of this Agreement may be effected only after amendment to this Agreement under Article XXVIII.

ARTICLE XI

Relations with Non-Member Countries

Section 1. *Undertakings regarding relations with non-member countries*

Each member undertakes:

(i) not to engage in, nor to permit any of its fiscal agencies referred to in Article V, Section 1 to engage in, any transactions with a non-member or with persons in a non-member's territories which would be contrary to the provisions of this Agreement or the purposes of the Fund;

(ii) not to cooperate with a non-member or with persons in a non-member's territories in practices which would be contrary to the provisions of this Agreement or the purposes of the Fund; and

(iii) to cooperate with the Fund with a view to the application in its territories of appropriate measures to prevent transactions with non-members or with persons in their territories which would be contrary to the provisions of this Agreement or the purposes of the Fund.

Section 2. *Restrictions on transactions with non-member countries*

Nothing in this Agreement shall affect the right of any member to impose restrictions on exchange transactions with non-members or with persons in their territories unless the Fund finds that such restrictions prejudice the interests of members and are contrary to the purposes of the Fund.

ARTICLE XII

Organization and Management

Section 1. *Structure of the Fund*

The Fund shall have a Board of Governors, an Executive Board, a Managing Director, and a staff, and a Council if the Board of Governors decides, by an eighty-five percent majority of the total voting power, that the provisions of Schedule D shall be applied.

Section 2. *Board of Governors*

(*a*) All powers under this Agreement not conferred directly on the Board of Governors, the Executive Board, or the Managing Director shall be vested in the Board of Governors. The Board of Governors shall consist of one Governor and one Alternate appointed by each member in such manner as it may determine. Each Governor and each Alternate shall serve until a new appointment is made. No Alternate may vote except in the absence of his principal. The Board of Governors shall select one of the Governors as Chairman.

(*b*) The Board of Governors may delegate to the Executive Board authority to exercise any powers of the Board of Governors, except the powers conferred directly by this Agreement on the Board of Governors.

(*c*) The Board of Governors shall hold such meetings as may be provided for by the Board of Governors or called by the Executive Board. Meetings of the Board of Governors shall be called whenever requested by fifteen members or by members having one-quarter of the total voting power.

(*d*) A quorum for any meeting of the Board of Governors shall be a majority of the Governors having not less than two-thirds of the total voting power.

(*e*) Each Governor shall be entitled to cast the number of votes allotted under Section 5 of this Article to the member appointing him.

(*f*) The Board of Governors may by regulation establish a procedure whereby the Executive Board, when it deems such action to be in the best interests of the Fund, may obtain a vote of the Governors on a specific question without calling a meeting of the Board of Governors.

(*g*) The Board of Governors, and the Executive Board to the extent authorized, may adopt such rules and regulations as may be necessary or appropriate to conduct the business of the Fund.

(*h*) Governors and Alternates shall serve as such without compensation from the Fund, but the Fund may pay them reasonable expenses incurred in attending meetings.

(*i*) The Board of Governors shall determine the remuneration to be paid to the Executive Directors and their Alternates and the salary and terms of the contract of service of the Managing Director.

(*j*) The Board of Governors and the Executive Board may appoint such committees as they deem advisable. Membership of committees need not be limited to Governors or Executive Directors or their Alternates.

Section 3. *Executive Board*

(*a*) The Executive Board shall be responsible for conducting the business of the Fund, and for this purpose shall exercise all the powers delegated to it by the Board of Governors.

(*b*) The Executive Board shall consist of Executive Directors with the Managing Director as chairman. Of the Executive Directors:

(i) five shall be appointed by the five members having the largest quotas; and

(ii) fifteen shall be elected by the other members.

For the purpose of each regular election of Executive Directors, the Board of Governors, by an eighty-five percent majority of the total voting power, may increase or decrease the number of Executive Directors in (ii) above. The number of Executive Directors in (ii) above shall be reduced by one or two, as the case may be, if Executive Directors are appointed under (*c*) below, unless the Board of Governors decides, by an eighty-five percent majority of the total voting power, that this reduction would hinder the effective discharge of the functions of the Executive Board or of Executive Directors or would threaten to upset a desirable balance in the Executive Board.

(*c*) If, at the second regular election of Executive Directors and thereafter, the members entitled to appoint Executive Directors under (*b*)(i) above do not include the two members, the holdings of whose currencies by the Fund in the General Resources Account have been, on the average over the preceding two years, reduced below their quotas by the largest absolute amounts in terms of the special drawing right, either one or both of such members, as the case may be, may appoint an Executive Director.

(*d*) Elections of elective Executive Directors shall be conducted at intervals of two years in accordance with the provisions of Schedule E, supplemented by such regulations as the Fund deems appropriate. For each regular election of Executive Directors, the Board of Governors may issue regulations making changes in the proportion of votes required to elect Executive Directors under the provisions of Schedule E.

(*e*) Each Executive Director shall appoint an Alternate with full power to act for him when he is not present. When the Executive Directors appointing them are present, Alternates may participate in meetings but may not vote.

(*f*) Executive Directors shall continue in office until their successors are appointed or elected. If the office of an elected Executive Director becomes vacant more than ninety days before the end of his term, another Executive Director shall be elected for the remainder of the term by the members that elected the former Executive Director. A majority of the votes cast shall be required for election. While the office remains vacant, the Alternate of the former Executive Director shall exercise his powers, except that of appointing an Alternate.

(*g*) The Executive Board shall function in continuous session at the principal office of the Fund and shall meet as often as the business of the Fund may require.

(*h*) A quorum for any meeting of the Executive Board shall be a majority of the Executive Directors having not less than one-half of the total voting power.

(*i*) (i) Each appointed Executive Director shall be entitled to cast the number of votes allotted under Section 5 of this Article to the member appointing him.

(ii) If the votes allotted to a member that appoints an Executive Director under (*c*) above were cast by an Executive Director together with the votes allotted to other members as a result of the last regular election of Executive

Directors, the member may agree with each of the other members that the number of votes allotted to it shall be cast by the appointed Executive Director. A member making such an agreement shall not participate in the election of Executive Directors.

(iii) Each elected Executive Director shall be entitled to cast the number of votes which counted towards his election.

(iv) When the provisions of Section 5(*b*) of this Article are applicable, the votes which an Executive Director would otherwise be entitled to cast shall be increased or decreased correspondingly. All the votes which an Executive Director is entitled to cast shall be cast as a unit.

(v) When the suspension of the voting rights of a member is terminated under Article XXVI, Section 2(*b*), and the member is not entitled to appoint an Executive Director, the member may agree with all the members that have elected an Executive Director that the number of votes allotted to that member shall be cast by such Executive Director, provided that, if no regular election of Executive Directors has been conducted during the period of the suspension, the Executive Director in whose election the member had participated prior to the suspension, or his successor elected in accordance with paragraph 3(*c*)(i) of Schedule L or with (*f*) above, shall be entitled to cast the number of votes allotted to the member. The member shall be deemed to have participated in the election of the Executive Director entitled to cast the number of votes allotted to the member.

(*j*) The Board of Governors shall adopt regulations under which a member not entitled to appoint an Executive Director under (*b*) above may send a representative to attend any meeting of the Executive Board when a request made by, or a matter particularly affecting, that member is under consideration.

Section 4. *Managing Director and staff*

(*a*) The Executive Board shall select a Managing Director who shall not be a Governor or an Executive Director. The Managing Director shall be chairman of the Executive Board, but shall have no vote except a deciding vote in case of an equal division. He may participate in meetings of the Board of Governors, but shall not vote at such meetings. The Managing Director shall cease to hold office when the Executive Board so decides.

(*b*) The Managing Director shall be chief of the operating staff of the Fund and shall conduct, under the direction of the Executive Board, the ordinary business of the Fund. Subject to the general control of the Executive Board, he shall be responsible for the organization, appointment, and dismissal of the staff of the Fund.

(*c*) The Managing Director and the staff of the Fund, in the discharge of their functions, shall owe their duty entirely to the Fund and to no other authority. Each member of the Fund shall respect the international character of this duty and shall refrain from all attempts to influence any of the staff in the discharge of these functions.

(*d*) In appointing the staff the Managing Director shall, subject to the paramount importance of securing the highest standards of efficiency and of technical competence, pay due regard to the importance of recruiting personnel on as wide a geographical basis as possible.

Section 5. *Voting*

(*a*) Each member shall have two hundred fifty votes plus one additional vote for each part of its quota equivalent to one hundred thousand special drawing rights.

(*b*) Whenever voting is required under Article V, Section 4 or 5, each member shall have the number of votes to which it is entitled under (*a*) above adjusted

(i) by the addition of one vote for the equivalent of each four hundred thousand special drawing rights of net sales of its currency from the general resources of the Fund up to the date when the vote is taken, or

(ii) by the subtraction of one vote for the equivalent of each four hundred thousand special drawing rights of its net purchases under Article V, Section 3(*b*) and (*f*) up to the date when the vote is taken,

provided that neither net purchases nor net sales shall be deemed at any time to exceed an amount equal to the quota of the member involved.

(*c*) Except as otherwise specifically provided, all decisions of the Fund shall be made by a majority of the votes cast.

Section 6. *Reserves, distribution of net income, and investment*

(*a*) The Fund shall determine annually what part of its net income shall be placed to general reserve or special reserve, and what part, if any, shall be distributed.

(*b*) The Fund may use the special reserve for any purpose for which it may use the general reserve, except distribution.

(*c*) If any distribution is made of the net income of any year, it shall be made to all members in proportion to their quotas.

(*d*) The Fund, by a seventy percent majority of the total voting power, may decide at any time to distribute any part of the general reserve. Any such distribution shall be made to all members in proportion to their quotas.

(*e*) Payments under (*c*) and (*d*) above shall be made in special drawing rights, provided that either the Fund or the member may decide that the payment to the member shall be made in its own currency.

(*f*) (i) The Fund may establish an Investment Account for the purposes of this subsection (*f*). The assets of the Investment Account shall be held separately from the other accounts of the General Department.

(ii) The Fund may decide to transfer to the Investment Account a part of the proceeds of the sale of gold in accordance with Article V, Section 12(*g*) and, by a seventy percent majority of the total voting power, may decide to transfer to the Investment Account, for immediate investment, currencies held in the General Resources Account. The amount of these transfers shall not exceed the total amount of the general reserve and the special reserve at the time of the decision.

(iii) The Fund may invest a member's currency held in the Investment Account in marketable obligations of that member or in marketable obligations of international financial organizations. No investment shall be made without the concurrence of the member whose currency is used to make the investment. The Fund shall invest only in obligations denominated in special drawing rights or in the currency used for investment.

(iv) The income of investment may be invested in accordance with the provisions of this subsection (*f*). Income not invested shall be held in the Investment Account or may be used for meeting the expenses of conducting the business of the Fund.

(v) The Fund may use a member's currency held in the Investment Account to obtain the currencies needed to meet the expenses of conducting the business of the Fund.

(vi) The Investment Account shall be terminated in the event of liquidation of the Fund and may be terminated, or the amount of the investment may be reduced, prior to liquidation of the Fund by a seventy percent majority of the total voting power. The Fund, by a seventy percent majority of the total voting power, shall adopt rules and regulations regarding administration of the Investment Account, which shall be consistent with (vii), (viii), and (ix) below.

(vii) Upon termination of the Investment Account because of liquidation of the Fund, any assets in this account shall be distributed in accordance with the provisions of Schedule K, provided that a portion of these assets corresponding to the proportion of the assets transferred to this account under Article V, Section 12(*g*) to the total of the assets transferred to this account shall be deemed to be assets held in the Special Disbursement Account and shall be distributed in accordance with Schedule K, paragraph 2(*a*)(ii).

(viii) Upon termination of the Investment Account prior to liquidation of the Fund, a portion of the assets held in this account corresponding to the proportion of the assets transferred to this account under Article V, Section 12(*g*) to the total of the assets transferred to the account shall be transferred to the Special Disbursement Account if it has not been terminated, and the balance of the assets held in the Investment Account shall be transferred to the General Resources Account for immediate use in operations and transactions.

(ix) On a reduction of the amount of the investment by the Fund, a portion of the reduction corresponding to the proportion of the assets transferred to the Investment Account under Article V, Section 12(*g*) to the total of the assets transferred to this account shall be transferred to the Special Disbursement Account if it has not been terminated, and the balance of the reduction shall be transferred to the General Resources Account for immediate use in operations and transactions.

Section 7. *Publication of reports*

(*a*) The Fund shall publish an annual report containing an audited statement of its accounts, and shall issue, at intervals of three months or less, a summary statement of its operations and transactions and its holdings of special drawing rights, gold, and currencies of members.

(*b*) The Fund may publish such other reports as it deems desirable for carrying out its purposes.

Section 8. *Communication of views to members*

The Fund shall at all times have the right to communicate its views informally to any member on any matter arising under this Agreement. The Fund may, by a seventy percent majority of the total voting power, decide to publish a report made to a member regarding its monetary or economic conditions and developments which directly tend to produce a serious disequilibrium in the international balance of payments of members. If the member is not entitled to appoint an Executive Director, it shall be entitled to representation in accordance with Section 3(*j*) of this Article. The Fund shall not publish a report involving changes in the fundamental structure of the economic organization of members.

Article XIII

Offices and Depositories

Section 1. *Location of offices*

The principal office of the Fund shall be located in the territory of the member having the largest quota, and agencies or branch offices may be established in the territories of other members.

Section 2. *Depositories*

(*a*) Each member shall designate its central bank as a depository for all the Fund's holdings of its currency, or if it has no central bank it shall designate such other institution as may be acceptable to the Fund.

(*b*) The Fund may hold other assets, including gold, in the depositories designated by the five members having the largest quotas and in such other designated depositories as the Fund may select. Initially, at least one-half of the holdings of the Fund shall be held in the depository designated by the member in whose territories the Fund has its principal office and at least forty percent shall be held in the depositories designated by the remaining four members referred to above. However, all transfers of gold by the Fund shall be made with due regard to the costs of transport and anticipated requirements of the Fund. In an emergency the Executive Board may transfer all or any part of the Fund's gold holdings to any place where they can be adequately protected.

Section 3. *Guarantee of the Fund's assets*

Each member guarantees all assets of the Fund against loss resulting from failure or default on the part of the depository designated by it.

Article XIV

Transitional Arrangements

Section 1. *Notification to the Fund*

Each member shall notify the Fund whether it intends to avail itself of the transitional arrangements in Section 2 of this Article, or whether it is prepared to accept the obligations of Article VIII, Sections 2, 3, and 4. A member availing itself of the transitional arrangements shall notify the Fund as soon thereafter as it is prepared to accept these obligations.

Section 2. *Exchange restrictions*

A member that has notified the Fund that it intends to avail itself of transitional arrangements under this provision may, notwithstanding the provisions of any other articles of this Agreement, maintain and adapt to changing circumstances the restrictions on payments and transfers for current international transactions that were in effect on the date on which it became a member. Members shall, however, have continuous regard in their foreign exchange policies to the purposes of the Fund, and, as soon as conditions permit, they shall take all possible measures to develop such commercial and financial arrangements with other members as will facilitate international payments and the promotion of a stable system of exchange rates. In particular, members shall withdraw restrictions maintained under this Section as soon as they are satisfied that they will be able, in the absence of such restrictions, to settle their balance of payments in a manner which will not unduly encumber their access to the general resources of the Fund.

Section 3. *Action of the Fund relating to restrictions*

The Fund shall make annual reports on the restrictions in force under Section 2 of this Article. Any member retaining any restrictions inconsistent with Article VIII, Sections 2, 3, or 4 shall consult the Fund annually as to their further retention. The Fund may, if it deems such action necessary in exceptional circumstances, make representations to any member that conditions are favorable for the withdrawal of any particular restriction, or for the general abandonment of restrictions, inconsistent with the provisions of any other articles of this Agreement. The member shall be given a suitable time to reply to such representations. If the Fund finds that the member persists in maintaining restrictions which are inconsistent with the purposes of the Fund, the member shall be subject to Article XXVI, Section 2(*a*).

Article XV

Special Drawing Rights

Section 1. *Authority to allocate special drawing rights*

To meet the need, as and when it arises, for a supplement to existing reserve assets, the Fund is authorized to allocate special drawing rights to members that are participants in the Special Drawing Rights Department.

Section 2. *Valuation of the special drawing right*

The method of valuation of the special drawing right shall be determined by the Fund by a seventy percent majority of the total voting power, provided, however, that an eighty-five percent majority of the total voting power shall be required for a change in the principle of valuation or a fundamental change in the application of the principle in effect.

Article XVI

General Department and Special Drawing Rights Department

Section 1. *Separation of operations and transactions*

All operations and transactions involving special drawing rights shall be conducted through the Special Drawing Rights Department. All other operations and transactions on the account of the Fund authorized by or under this Agreement shall be conducted through the General Department. Operations and transactions pursuant to Article XVII, Section 2 shall be conducted through the General Department as well as the Special Drawing Rights Department.

Section 2. *Separation of assets and property*

All assets and property of the Fund, except resources administered under Article V, Section 2(*b*), shall be held in the General Department, provided that assets and property acquired under Article XX, Section 2 and Articles XXIV and XXV and Schedules H and I shall be held in the Special Drawing Rights Department. Any assets or property held in one Department shall not be available to discharge or meet the liabilities, obligations, or losses of the Fund incurred in the conduct of the operations and transactions of the other Department, except that the expenses of conducting the business of the Special Drawing Rights Department shall be paid by the Fund from the General Department which shall be reimbursed in special drawing rights from time to time by assessments under Article XX, Section 4 made on the basis of a reasonable estimate of such expenses.

Section 3. *Recording and information*

All changes in holdings of special drawing rights shall take effect only when recorded by the Fund in the Special Drawing Rights Department. Participants shall notify the Fund of the provisions of this Agreement under which special drawing rights are used. The Fund may require participants to furnish it with such other information as it deems necessary for its functions.

ARTICLE XVII

Participants and Other Holders of Special Drawing Rights

Section 1. *Participants*

Each member of the Fund that deposits with the Fund an instrument setting forth that it undertakes all the obligations of a participant in the Special Drawing Rights Department in accordance with its law and that it has taken all steps necessary to enable it to carry out all of these obligations shall become a participant in the Special Drawing Rights Department as of the date the instrument is deposited, except that no member shall become a participant before the provisions of this Agreement pertaining exclusively to the Special Drawing Rights Department have entered into force and instruments have been deposited under this Section by members that have at least seventy-five percent of the total of quotas.

Section 2. *Fund as a holder*

The Fund may hold special drawing rights in the General Resources Account and may accept and use them in operations and transactions conducted through the General Resources Account with participants in accordance with the provisions of this Agreement or with prescribed holders in accordance with the terms and conditions prescribed under Section 3 of this Article.

Section 3. *Other holders*

The Fund may prescribe:

(i) as holders, non-members, members that are non-participants, institutions that perform functions of a central bank for more than one member, and other official entities;

(ii) the terms and conditions on which prescribed holders may be permitted to hold special drawing rights and may accept and use them in operations and transactions with participants and other prescribed holders; and

(iii) the terms and conditions on which participants and the Fund through the General Resources Account may enter into operations and transactions in special drawing rights with prescribed holders.

An eighty-five percent majority of the total voting power shall be required for prescriptions under (i) above. The terms and conditions prescribed by the Fund shall be consistent with the provisions of this Agreement and the effective functioning of the Special Drawing Rights Department.

Article XVIII

Allocation and Cancellation of Special Drawing Rights

Section 1. *Principles and considerations governing allocation and cancellation*

(*a*) In all its decisions with respect to the allocation and cancellation of special drawing rights the Fund shall seek to meet the long-term global need, as and when it arises, to supplement existing reserve assets in such manner as will promote the attainment of its purposes and will avoid economic stagnation and deflation as well as excess demand and inflation in the world.

(*b*) The first decision to allocate special drawing rights shall take into account, as special considerations, a collective judgment that there is a global need to supplement reserves, and the attainment of a better balance of payments equilibrium, as well as the likelihood of a better working of the adjustment process in the future.

Section 2. *Allocation and cancellation*

(*a*) Decisions of the Fund to allocate or cancel special drawing rights shall be made for basic periods which shall run consecutively and shall be five years in duration. The first basic period shall begin on the date of the first decision to allocate special drawing rights or such later date as may be specified in that decision. Any allocations or cancellations shall take place at yearly intervals.

(*b*) The rates at which allocations are to be made shall be expressed as percentages of quotas on the date of each decision to allocate. The rates at which special drawing rights are to be cancelled shall be expressed as percentages of net cumulative allocations of special drawing rights on the date of each decision to cancel. The percentages shall be the same for all participants.

(*c*) In its decision for any basic period the Fund may provide, notwithstanding (*a*) and (*b*) above, that:

(i) the duration of the basic period shall be other than five years; or

(ii) the allocations or cancellations shall take place at other than yearly intervals; or

(iii) the basis for allocations or cancellations shall be the quotas or net cumulative allocations on dates other than the dates of decisions to allocate or cancel.

(*d*) A member that becomes a participant after a basic period starts shall receive allocations beginning with the next basic period in which allocations are made after it becomes a participant unless the Fund decides that the new participant shall start to receive allocations beginning with the next allocation after it becomes a participant. If the Fund decides that a member that becomes a participant during a basic period shall receive allocations during the remainder of that basic period and the participant was not a member on the dates established under (*b*) or (*c*) above, the Fund shall determine the basis on which these allocations to the participant shall be made.

(*e*) A participant shall receive allocations of special drawing rights made pursuant to any decision to allocate unless:

(i) the Governor for the participant did not vote in favor of the decision; and

(ii) the participant has notified the Fund in writing prior to the first allocation of special drawing rights under that decision that it does not wish special drawing rights to be allocated to it under the decision. On the request of a participant, the Fund may decide to terminate the effect of the notice with respect to allocations of special drawing rights subsequent to the termination.

(*f*) If on the effective date of any cancellation the amount of special drawing rights held by a participant is less than its share of the special drawing rights that are to be cancelled, the participant shall eliminate its negative balance as promptly as its gross reserve position permits and shall remain in consultation with the Fund for this purpose. Special drawing rights acquired by the participant after the effective date of the cancellation shall be applied against its negative balance and cancelled.

Section 3. *Unexpected major developments*

The Fund may change the rates or intervals of allocation or cancellation during the rest of a basic period or change the length of a basic period or start a new basic period, if at any time the Fund finds it desirable to do so because of unexpected major developments.

Section 4. *Decisions on allocations and cancellations*

(*a*) Decisions under Section 2(*a*), (*b*), and (*c*) or Section 3 of this Article shall be made by the Board of Governors on the basis of proposals of the Managing Director concurred in by the Executive Board.

(*b*) Before making any proposal, the Managing Director, after having satisfied himself that it will be consistent with the provisions of Section 1(*a*) of this Article, shall conduct such consultations as will enable him to ascertain that there is broad support among participants for the proposal. In addition, before making a proposal for the first allocation, the Managing Director shall satisfy himself that the provisions of Section 1(*b*) of this Article have been met and that there is broad support among participants to begin allocations; he shall make a proposal for the first allocation as soon after the establishment of the Special Drawing Rights Department as he is so satisfied.

(*c*) The Managing Director shall make proposals:

(i) not later than six months before the end of each basic period;

(ii) if no decision has been taken with respect to allocation or cancellation for a basic period, whenever he is satisfied that the provisions of (*b*) above have been met;

(iii) when, in accordance with Section 3 of this Article, he considers that it would be desirable to change the rate or intervals of allocation or cancellation or change the length of a basic period or start a new basic period; or

(iv) within six months of a request by the Board of Governors or the Executive Board;

provided that, if under (i), (iii), or (iv) above the Managing Director ascertains that there is no proposal which he considers to be consistent with the provisions of Section 1 of this Article that has broad support among participants in accordance with (*b*) above, he shall report to the Board of Governors and to the Executive Board.

(*d*) An eighty-five percent majority of the total voting power shall be required for decisions under Section 2(*a*), (*b*), and (*c*) or Section 3 of this Article except for decisions under Section 3 with respect to a decrease in the rates of allocation.

ARTICLE XIX

Operations and Transactions in Special Drawing Rights

Section 1. *Use of special drawing rights*

Special drawing rights may be used in the operations and transactions authorized by or under this Agreement.

Section 2. *Operations and transactions between participants*

(*a*) A participant shall be entitled to use its special drawing rights to obtain an equivalent amount of currency from a participant designated under Section 5 of this Article.

(*b*) A participant, in agreement with another participant, may use its special drawing rights to obtain an equivalent amount of currency from the other participant.

(*c*) The Fund, by a seventy percent majority of the total voting power, may prescribe operations in which a participant is authorized to engage in agreement with another participant on such terms and conditions as the Fund deems appropriate. The terms and conditions shall be consistent with the effective functioning of the Special Drawing Rights Department and the proper use of special drawing rights in accordance with this Agreement.

(*d*) The Fund may make representations to a participant that enters into any operation or transaction under (*b*) or (*c*) above that in the judgment of the Fund may be prejudicial to the process of designation according to the principles of Section 5 of this Article or is otherwise inconsistent with Article XXII. A participant that persists in entering into such operations or transactions shall be subject to Article XXIII, Section 2(*b*).

Section 3. *Requirement of need*

(*a*) In transactions under Section 2(*a*) of this Article, except as otherwise provided in (*c*) below, a participant will be expected to use its special drawing rights only if it has a need because of its balance of payments or its reserve position or developments in its reserves, and not for the sole purpose of changing the composition of its reserves.

(*b*) The use of special drawing rights shall not be subject to challenge on the basis of the expectation in (*a*) above, but the Fund may make representations to a participant that fails to fulfill this expectation. A participant that persists in failing to fulfill this expectation shall be subject to Article XXIII, Section 2(*b*).

(*c*) The Fund may waive the expectation in (*a*) above in any transactions in which a participant uses special drawing rights to obtain an equivalent amount of currency from a participant designated under Section 5 of this Article that would promote reconstitution by the other participant under Section 6(*a*) of this Article; prevent or reduce a negative balance of the other participant; or offset the effect of a failure by the other participant to fulfill the expectation in (*a*) above.

Section 4. *Obligation to provide currency*

(*a*) A participant designated by the Fund under Section 5 of this Article shall provide on demand a freely usable currency to a participant using special drawing rights under Section 2(*a*) of this Article. A participant's obligation to provide currency shall not extend beyond the point at which its holdings of special drawing rights in excess of its net cumulative allocation are equal to twice its net cumulative allocation or such higher limit as may be agreed between a participant and the Fund.

(*b*) A participant may provide currency in excess of the obligatory limit or any agreed higher limit.

Section 5. *Designation of participants to provide currency*

(*a*) The Fund shall ensure that a participant will be able to use its special drawing rights by designating participants to provide currency for specified amounts of special drawing rights for the purposes of Sections 2(*a*) and 4 of this Article. Designations shall be made in accordance with the following general principles supplemented by such other principles as the Fund may adopt from time to time:

(i) A participant shall be subject to designation if its balance of payments and gross reserve position is sufficiently strong, but this will not preclude the possibility that a participant with a strong reserve position will be designated even though it has a moderate balance of payments deficit. Participants shall be designated in such manner as will promote over time a balanced distribution of holdings of special drawing rights among them.

(ii) Participants shall be subject to designation in order to promote reconstitution under Section 6(*a*) of this Article, to reduce negative balances in holdings of special drawing rights, or to offset the effect of failures to fulfill the expectation in Section 3(*a*) of this Article.

(iii) In designating participants, the Fund normally shall give priority to those that need to acquire special drawing rights to meet the objectives of designation under (ii) above.

(*b*) In order to promote over time a balanced distribution of holdings of special drawing rights under (*a*)(i) above, the Fund shall apply the rules for designation in Schedule F or such rules as may be adopted under (*c*) below.

(*c*) The rules for designation may be reviewed at any time and new rules shall be adopted if necessary. Unless new rules are adopted, the rules in force at the time of the review shall continue to apply.

Section 6. *Reconstitution*

(*a*) Participants that use their special drawing rights shall reconstitute their holdings of them in accordance with the rules for reconstitution in Schedule G or such rules as may be adopted under (*b*) below.

(*b*) The rules for reconstitution may be reviewed at any time and new rules shall be adopted if necessary. Unless new rules are adopted or a decision is made to abrogate rules for reconstitution, the rules in force at the time of review shall continue to apply. A seventy percent majority of the total voting power shall be required for decisions to adopt, modify, or abrogate the rules for reconstitution.

Section 7. *Exchange rates*

(*a*) Except as otherwise provided in (*b*) below, the exchange rates for transactions between participants under Section 2(*a*) and (*b*) of this Article shall be such that participants using special drawing rights shall receive the same value whatever currencies might be provided and whichever participants provide those currencies, and the Fund shall adopt regulations to give effect to this principle.

(*b*) The Fund, by an eighty-five percent majority of the total voting power, may adopt policies under which in exceptional circumstances the Fund, by a seventy percent majority of the total voting power, may authorize participants entering into transactions under Section 2(*b*) of this Article to agree on exchange rates other than those applicable under (*a*) above.

(*c*) The Fund shall consult a participant on the procedure for determining rates of exchange for its currency.

(*d*) For the purpose of this provision the term participant includes a terminating participant.

Article XX

Special Drawing Rights Department Interest and Charges

Section 1. *Interest*

Interest at the same rate for all holders shall be paid by the Fund to each holder on the amount of its holdings of special drawing rights. The Fund shall pay the amount due to each holder whether or not sufficient charges are received to meet the payment of interest.

Section 2. *Charges*

Charges at the same rate for all participants shall be paid to the Fund by each participant on the amount of its net cumulative allocation of special drawing rights plus any negative balance of the participant or unpaid charges.

Section 3. *Rate of interest and charges*

The Fund shall determine the rate of interest by a seventy percent majority of the total voting power. The rate of charges shall be equal to the rate of interest.

Section 4. *Assessments*

When it is decided under Article XVI, Section 2 that reimbursement shall be made, the Fund shall levy assessments for this purpose at the same rate for all participants on their net cumulative allocations.

Section 5. *Payment of interest, charges, and assessments*

Interest, charges, and assessments shall be paid in special drawing rights. A participant that needs special drawing rights to pay any charge or assessment shall be obligated and entitled to obtain them, for currency acceptable to the Fund, in a transaction with the Fund conducted through the General Resources Account. If sufficient special drawing rights cannot be obtained in this way, the participant shall be obligated and entitled to obtain them with a freely usable currency from a participant which the Fund shall specify. Special drawing rights acquired by a participant after the date for payment shall be applied against its unpaid charges and cancelled.

Article XXI

Administration of the General Department and the Special Drawing Rights Department

(*a*) The General Department and the Special Drawing Rights Department shall be administered in accordance with the provisions of Article XII, subject to the following provisions:

(i) For meetings of or decisions by the Board of Governors on matters pertaining exclusively to the Special Drawing Rights Department only requests by, or the presence and the votes of, Governors appointed by members that are participants shall be counted for the purpose of calling meetings and determining whether a quorum exists or whether a decision is made by the required majority.

(ii) For decisions by the Executive Board on matters pertaining exclusively to the Special Drawing Rights Department only Executive Directors appointed or elected by at least one member that is a participant shall be entitled to vote. Each of these Executive Directors shall be entitled to cast the number of votes allotted to the member which is a participant that appointed him or to the members that are participants whose votes counted towards his election. Only the presence of Executive Directors appointed or elected by members that are participants and the votes allotted to members that are participants shall be counted for the purpose of determining whether a quorum exists or whether a decision is made by the required majority. For the purposes of this provision, an agreement under Article XII, Section 3(*i*)(ii) by a member that is a participant shall entitle an appointed Executive Director to vote and cast the number of votes allotted to the member.

(iii) Questions of the general administration of the Fund, including reimbursement under Article XVI, Section 2, and any question whether a matter pertains to both Departments or exclusively to the Special Drawing Rights Department shall be decided as if they pertained exclusively to the General Department. Decisions with respect to the method of valuation of the special drawing right, the acceptance and holding of special drawing rights in the General Resources Account of the General

Department and the use of them, and other decisions affecting the operations and transactions conducted through both the General Resources Account of the General Department and the Special Drawing Rights Department shall be made by the majorities required for decisions on matters pertaining exclusively to each Department. A decision on a matter pertaining to the Special Drawing Rights Department shall so indicate.

(*b*) In addition to the privileges and immunities that are accorded under Article IX of this Agreement, no tax of any kind shall be levied on special drawing rights or on operations or transactions in special drawing rights.

(*c*) A question of interpretation of the provisions of this Agreement on matters pertaining exclusively to the Special Drawing Rights Department shall be submitted to the Executive Board pursuant to Article XXIX(*a*) only on the request of a participant. In any case where the Executive Board has given a decision on a question of interpretation pertaining exclusively to the Special Drawing Rights Department only a participant may require that the question be referred to the Board of Governors under Article XXIX(*b*). The Board of Governors shall decide whether a Governor appointed by a member that is not a participant shall be entitled to vote in the Committee on Interpretation on questions pertaining exclusively to the Special Drawing Rights Department.

(*d*) Whenever a disagreement arises between the Fund and a participant that has terminated its participation in the Special Drawing Rights Department or between the Fund and any participant during the liquidation of the Special Drawing Rights Department with respect to any matter arising exclusively from participation in the Special Drawing Rights Department, the disagreement shall be submitted to arbitration in accordance with the procedures in Article XXIX(*c*).

Article XXII

General Obligations of Participants

In addition to the obligations assumed with respect to special drawing rights under other articles of this Agreement, each participant undertakes to collaborate with the Fund and with other participants in order to facilitate the effective functioning of the Special Drawing

Rights Department and the proper use of special drawing rights in accordance with this Agreement and with the objective of making the special drawing right the principal reserve asset in the international monetary system.

Article XXIII

Suspension of Operations and Transactions in Special Drawing Rights

Section 1. *Emergency provisions*

In the event of an emergency or the development of unforeseen circumstances threatening the activities of the Fund with respect to the Special Drawing Rights Department, the Executive Board, by an eighty-five percent majority of the total voting power, may suspend for a period of not more than one year the operation of any of the provisions relating to operations and transactions in special drawing rights, and the provisions of Article XXVII, Section 1(*b*), (*c*), and (*d*) shall then apply.

Section 2. *Failure to fulfill obligations*

(*a*) If the Fund finds that a participant has failed to fulfill its obligations under Article XIX, Section 4, the right of the participant to use its special drawing rights shall be suspended unless the Fund otherwise decides.

(*b*) If the Fund finds that a participant has failed to fulfill any other obligation with respect to special drawing rights, the Fund may suspend the right of the participant to use special drawing rights it acquires after the suspension.

(*c*) Regulations shall be adopted to ensure that before action is taken against any participant under (*a*) or (*b*) above, the participant shall be informed immediately of the complaint against it and given an adequate opportunity for stating its case, both orally and in writing. Whenever the participant is thus informed of a complaint relating to (*a*) above, it shall not use special drawing rights pending the disposition of the complaint.

(*d*) Suspension under (*a*) or (*b*) above or limitation under (*c*) above shall not affect a participant's obligation to provide currency in accordance with Article XIX, Section 4.

(*e*) The Fund may at any time terminate a suspension under (*a*) or (*b*) above, provided that a suspension imposed on a participant under (*b*) above for failure to fulfill the obligations under Article XIX, Section 6(*a*) shall not be terminated until one hundred eighty days after the end of the first calendar quarter during which the participant complies with the rules for reconstitution.

(*f*) The right of a participant to use its special drawing rights shall not be suspended because it has become ineligible to use the Fund's general resources under Article V, Section 5, Article VI, Section 1, or Article XXVI, Section 2(*a*). Article XXVI, Section 2 shall not apply because a participant has failed to fulfill any obligations with respect to special drawing rights.

Article XXIV

Termination of Participation

Section 1. *Right to terminate participation*

(*a*) Any participant may terminate its participation in the Special Drawing Rights Department at any time by transmitting a notice in writing to the Fund at its principal office. Termination shall become effective on the date the notice is received.

(*b*) A participant that withdraws from membership in the Fund shall be deemed to have simultaneously terminated its participation in the Special Drawing Rights Department.

Section 2. *Settlement on termination*

(*a*) When a participant terminates its participation in the Special Drawing Rights Department, all operations and transactions by the terminating participant in special drawing rights shall cease except as otherwise permitted under an agreement made pursuant to (*c*) below in order to facilitate a settlement or as provided in Sections 3, 5, and 6 of this Article or in Schedule H. Interest and charges that accrued to the date of termination and assessments levied before that date but not paid shall be paid in special drawing rights.

(*b*) The Fund shall be obligated to redeem all special drawing rights held by the terminating participant, and the terminating participant shall be obligated to pay to the Fund an amount equal to its net cumulative allocation and any other amounts that may be due and payable because of its participation in the Special Drawing

Rights Department. These obligations shall be set off against each other and the amount of special drawing rights held by the terminating participant that is used in the setoff to extinguish its obligation to the fund shall be cancelled.

(*c*) A settlement shall be made with reasonable despatch by agreement between the terminating participant and the Fund with respect to any obligation of the terminating participant or the Fund after the setoff in (*b*) above. If agreement on a settlement is not reached promptly the provisions of Schedule H shall apply.

Section 3. *Interest and charges*

After the date of termination the Fund shall pay interest on any outstanding balance of special drawing rights held by a terminating participant and the terminating participant shall pay charges on any outstanding obligation owed to the Fund at the times and rates prescribed under Article XX. Payment shall be made in special drawing rights. A terminating participant shall be entitled to obtain special drawing rights with a freely usable currency to pay charges or assessments in a transaction with a participant specified by the Fund or by agreement from any other holder, or to dispose of special drawing rights received as interest in a transaction with any participant designated under Article XIX, Section 5 or by agreement with any other holder.

Section 4. *Settlement of obligation to the Fund*

Currency received by the Fund from a terminating participant shall be used by the Fund to redeem special drawing rights held by participants in proportion to the amount by which each participant's holdings of special drawing rights exceed its net cumulative allocation at the time the currency is received by the Fund. Special drawing rights so redeemed and special drawing rights obtained by a terminating participant under the provisions of this Agreement to meet any installment due under an agreement on settlement or under Schedule H and set off against that installment shall be cancelled.

Section 5. *Settlement of obligation to a terminating participant*

Whenever the Fund is required to redeem special drawing rights held by a terminating participant, redemption shall be made with currency provided by participants specified by the Fund. These participants shall be specified in accordance with the principles in Article XIX, Section 5. Each specified participant shall provide at its option the currency of the terminating participant or a freely usable currency to the Fund and shall receive an equivalent amount of special drawing rights. However, a terminating participant may use its special drawing rights to obtain its own currency, a freely usable currency, or any other asset from any holder, if the Fund so permits.

Section 6. *General Resources Account transactions*

In order to facilitate settlement with a terminating participant, the Fund may decide that a terminating participant shall:

(i) use any special drawing rights held by it after the setoff in Section 2(*b*) of this Article, when they are to be redeemed, in a transaction with the Fund conducted through the General Resources Account to obtain its own currency or a freely usable currency at the option of the Fund; or

(ii) obtain special drawing rights in a transaction with the Fund conducted through the General Resources Account for a currency acceptable to the Fund to meet any charges or installment due under an agreement or the provisions of Schedule H.

ARTICLE XXV

Liquidation of the Special Drawing Rights Department

(*a*) The Special Drawing Rights Department may not be liquidated except by decision of the Board of Governors. In an emergency, if the Executive Board decides that liquidation of the Special Drawing Rights Department may be necessary, it may temporarily suspend allocations or cancellations and all operations and transactions in special drawing rights pending decision by the Board of Governors. A decision by the Board of Governors to liquidate the Fund shall be a decision to liquidate both the General Department and the Special Drawing Rights Department.

(*b*) If the Board of Governors decides to liquidate the Special Drawing Rights Department, all allocations or cancellations and all operations and transactions in special drawing rights and the activities of the Fund with respect to the Special Drawing Rights Department shall cease except those incidental to the orderly discharge of the obligations of participants and of the Fund with respect to special drawing rights, and all obligations of the Fund and of participants under this Agreement with respect to special drawing rights shall cease except those set out in this Article, Article XX, Article XXI(*d*), Article XXIV, Article XXIX(*c*), and Schedule H, or any agreement reached under Article XXIV subject to paragraph 4 of Schedule H, and Schedule I.

(*c*) Upon liquidation of the Special Drawing Rights Department, interest and charges that accrued to the date of liquidation and assessments levied before that date but not paid shall be paid in special drawing rights. The Fund shall be obligated to redeem all special drawing rights held by holders, and each participant shall be obligated to pay the Fund an amount equal to its net cumulative allocation of special drawing rights and such other amounts as may be due and payable because of its participation in the Special Drawing Rights Department.

(*d*) Liquidation of the Special Drawing Rights Department shall be administered in accordance with the provisions of Schedule I.

ARTICLE XXVI

Withdrawal from Membership

Section 1. *Right of members to withdraw*

Any member may withdraw from the Fund at any time by transmitting a notice in writing to the Fund at its principal office. Withdrawal shall become effective on the date such notice is received.

Section 2. *Compulsory withdrawal*

(*a*) If a member fails to fulfill any of its obligations under this Agreement, the Fund may declare the member ineligible to use the general resources of the Fund. Nothing in this Section shall be deemed to limit the provisions of Article V, Section 5 or Article VI, Section 1.

(*b*) If, after the expiration of a reasonable period following a declaration of ineligibility under (*a*) above, the member persists in its failure to fulfill any of its obligations under this Agreement, the Fund may, by a seventy percent majority of the total voting power, suspend the voting rights of the member. During the period of the suspension, the provisions of Schedule L shall apply. The Fund may, by a seventy percent majority of the total voting power, terminate the suspension at any time.

(*c*) If, after the expiration of a reasonable period following a decision of suspension under (*b*) above, the member persists in its failure to fulfill any of its obligations under this Agreement, that member may be required to withdraw from membership in the Fund by a decision of the Board of Governors carried by a majority of the Governors having eighty-five percent of the total voting power.

(*d*) Regulations shall be adopted to ensure that before action is taken against any member under (*a*), (*b*), or (*c*) above, the member shall be informed in reasonable time of the complaint against it and given an adequate opportunity for stating its case, both orally and in writing.

Section 3. *Settlement of accounts with members withdrawing*

When a member withdraws from the Fund, normal operations and transactions of the Fund in its currency shall cease and settlement of all accounts between it and the Fund shall be made with reasonable despatch by agreement between it and the Fund. If agreement is not reached promptly, the provisions of Schedule J shall apply to the settlement of accounts.

Article XXVII

Emergency Provisions

Section 1. *Temporary suspension*

(*a*) In the event of an emergency or the development of unforeseen circumstances threatening the activities of the Fund, the Executive Board, by an eighty-five percent majority of the total voting power, may suspend for a period of not more than one year the operation of any of the following provisions:

(i) Article V, Sections 2, 3, 7, 8(*a*)(i) and (*e*);

(ii) Article VI, Section 2;

(iii) Article XI, Section 1;

(iv) Schedule C, paragraph 5.

(*b*) A suspension of the operation of a provision under (*a*) above may not be extended beyond one year except by the Board of Governors which, by an eighty-five percent majority of the total voting power, may extend a suspension for an additional period of not more than two years if it finds that the emergency or unforeseen circumstances referred to in (*a*) above continue to exist.

(*c*) The Executive Board may, by a majority of the total voting power, terminate such suspension at any time.

(*d*) The Fund may adopt rules with respect to the subject matter of a provision during the period in which its operation is suspended.

Section 2. *Liquidation of the Fund*

(*a*) The Fund may not be liquidated except by decision of the Board of Governors. In an emergency, if the Executive Board decides that liquidation of the Fund may be necessary, it may temporarily suspend all operations and transactions, pending decision by the Board of Governors.

(*b*) If the Board of Governors decides to liquidate the Fund, the Fund shall forthwith cease to engage in any activities except those incidental to the orderly collection and liquidation of its assets and the settlement of its liabilities, and all obligations of members under this Agreement shall cease except those set out in this Article, in Article XXIX(*c*), in Schedule J, paragraph 7, and in Schedule K.

(*c*) Liquidation shall be administered in accordance with the provisions of Schedule K.

Article XXVIII

Amendments

(*a*) Any proposal to introduce modifications in this Agreement, whether emanating from a member, a Governor, or the Executive Board, shall be communicated to the chairman of the Board of Governors who shall bring the proposal before the Board of Governors. If the proposed amendment is approved by the Board of Governors, the Fund shall, by circular letter or telegram, ask all members whether they accept the proposed amendment. When three-fifths of the members, having eighty-five percent of the total voting power, have accepted the proposed amendment, the Fund shall certify the fact by a formal communication addressed to all members.

(*b*) Notwithstanding (*a*) above, acceptance by all members is required in the case of any amendment modifying:

(i) the right to withdraw from the Fund (Article XXVI, Section 1);

(ii) the provision that no change in a member's quota shall be made without its consent (Article III, Section 2(*d*)); and

(iii) the provision that no change may be made in the par value of a member's currency except on the proposal of that member (Schedule C, paragraph 6).

(*c*) Amendments shall enter into force for all members three months after the date of the formal communication unless a shorter period is specified in the circular letter or telegram.

ARTICLE XXIX

Interpretation

(*a*) Any question of interpretation of the provisions of this Agreement arising between any member and the Fund or between any members of the Fund shall be submitted to the Executive Board for its decision. If the question particularly affects any member not entitled to appoint an Executive Director, it shall be entitled to representation in accordance with Article XII, Section 3(*j*).

(*b*) In any case where the Executive Board has given a decision under (*a*) above, any member may require, within three months from the date of the decision, that the question be referred to the Board of Governors, whose decision shall be final. Any question referred to the Board of Governors shall be considered by a Committee on Interpretation of the Board of Governors. Each Committee member shall have one vote. The Board of Governors shall establish the membership, procedures, and voting majorities of the Committee. A decision of the Committee shall be the decision of the Board of Governors unless the Board of Governors, by an eighty-five percent majority of the total voting power, decides otherwise. Pending the result of the reference to the Board of Governors the Fund may, so far as it deems necessary, act on the basis of the decision of the Executive Board.

(*c*) Whenever a disagreement arises between the Fund and a member which has withdrawn, or between the Fund and any member during liquidation of the Fund, such disagreement shall be submitted to arbitration by a tribunal of three arbitrators, one appointed by the Fund, another by the member or withdrawing member, and an umpire who, unless the parties otherwise agree, shall be appointed by the President of the International Court of Justice or such other authority as may have been prescribed by regulation adopted by the Fund. The umpire shall have full power to settle all questions of procedure in any case where the parties are in disagreement with respect thereto.

Article XXX

Explanation of Terms

In interpreting the provisions of this Agreement the Fund and its members shall be guided by the following provisions:

(*a*) The Fund's holdings of a member's currency in the General Resources Account shall include any securities accepted by the Fund under Article III, Section 4.

(*b*) Stand-by arrangement means a decision of the Fund by which a member is assured that it will be able to make purchases from the General Resources Account in accordance with the terms of the decision during a specified period and up to a specified amount.

(*c*) Reserve tranche purchase means a purchase by a member of special drawing rights or the currency of another member in exchange for its own currency which does not cause the Fund's holdings of the member's currency in the General Resources Account to exceed its quota, provided that for the purposes of this definition the Fund may exclude purchases and holdings under:

(i) policies on the use of its general resources for compensatory financing of export fluctuations;

(ii) policies on the use of its general resources in connection with the financing of contributions to international buffer stocks of primary products; and

(iii) other policies on the use of its general resources in respect of which the Fund decides, by an eighty-five percent majority of the total voting power, that an exclusion shall be made.

(*d*) Payments for current transactions means payments which are not for the purpose of transferring capital, and includes, without limitation:

(1) all payments due in connection with foreign trade, other current business, including services, and normal short-term banking and credit facilities;

(2) payments due as interest on loans and as net income from other investments;

(3) payments of moderate amount for amortization of loans or for depreciation of direct investments; and

(4) moderate remittances for family living expenses.

The Fund may, after consultation with the members concerned, determine whether certain specific transactions are to be considered current transactions or capital transactions.

(*e*) Net cumulative allocation of special drawing rights means the total amount of special drawing rights allocated to a participant less its share of special drawing rights that have been cancelled under Article XVIII, Section 2(*a*).

(*f*) A freely usable currency means a member's currency that the Fund determines (i) is, in fact, widely used to make payments for international transactions, and (ii) is widely traded in the principal exchange markets.

(*g*) Members that were members on August 31, 1975 shall be deemed to include a member that accepted membership after that date pursuant to a resolution of the Board of Governors adopted before that date.

(*h*) Transactions of the Fund means exchanges of monetary assets by the Fund for other monetary assets. Operations of the Fund means other uses or receipts of monetary assets by the Fund.

(*i*) Transactions in special drawing rights means exchanges of special drawing rights for other monetary assets. Operations in special drawing rights means other uses of special drawing rights.

ARTICLE XXXI

Final Provisions

Section 1. *Entry into force*

This Agreement shall enter into force when it has been signed on behalf of governments having sixty-five percent of the total of the quotas set forth in Schedule A and when the instruments referred to in Section 2(*a*) of this Article have been deposited on their behalf, but in no event shall this Agreement enter into force before May 1, 1945.

Section 2. *Signature*

(*a*) Each government on whose behalf this Agreement is signed shall deposit with the Government of the United States of America an instrument setting forth that it has accepted this Agreement in accordance with its law and has taken all steps necessary to enable it to carry out all of its obligations under this Agreement.

(*b*) Each country shall become a member of the Fund as from the date of the deposit on its behalf of the instrument referred to in (*a*) above, except that no country shall become a member before this Agreement enters into force under Section 1 of this Article.

(*c*) The Government of the United States of America shall inform the governments of all countries whose names are set forth in Schedule A, and the governments of all countries whose membership is approved in accordance with Article II, Section 2, of all signatures of this Agreement and of the deposit of all instruments referred to in (*a*) above.

(*d*) At the time this Agreement is signed on its behalf, each government shall transmit to the Government of the United States of America one one-hundredth of one percent of its total subscription in gold or United States dollars for the purpose of meeting administrative expenses of the Fund. The Government of the United States of America shall hold such funds in a special deposit account and shall transmit them to the Board of Governors of the Fund when the initial meeting has been called. If this Agreement has not come into force by December 31, 1945, the Government of the United States of America shall return such funds to the governments that transmitted them.

(*e*) This Agreement shall remain open for signature at Washington on behalf of the governments of the countries whose names are set forth in Schedule A until December 31, 1945.

(*f*) After December 31, 1945, this Agreement shall be open for signature on behalf of the government of any country whose membership has been approved in accordance with Article II, Section 2.

(*g*) By their signature of this Agreement, all governments accept it both on their own behalf and in respect of all their colonies, overseas territories, all territories under their protection, suzerainty, or authority, and all territories in respect of which they exercise a mandate.

(*h*) Subsection (*d*) above shall come into force with regard to each signatory government as from the date of its signature.

[The signature and depositary clause reproduced below followed the text of Article XX in the original Articles of Agreement]

Done at Washington, in a single copy which shall remain deposited in the archives of the Government of the United States of America, which shall transmit certified copies to all governments whose names are set forth in Schedule A and to all governments whose membership is approved in accordance with Article II, Section 2.

SCHEDULE A

Quotas

(In millions of United States dollars)

Australia	200	India	400
Belgium	225	Iran	25
Bolivia	10	Iraq	8
Brazil	150	Liberia	.5
Canada	300	Luxembourg	10
Chile	50	Mexico	90
China	550	Netherlands	275
Colombia	50	New Zealand	50
Costa Rica	5	Nicaragua	2
Cuba	50	Norway	50
Czechoslovakia	125	Panama	.5
Denmark*	*	Paraguay	2
Dominican Republic	5	Peru	25
Ecuador	5	Philippine Commonwealth	15
Egypt	45	Poland	125
El Salvador	2.5	Union of South Africa	100
Ethiopia	6	Union of Soviet Socialist Republics	1200
France	450	United Kingdom	1300
Greece	40	United States	2750
Guatemala	5	Uruguay	15
Haiti	5	Venezuela	15
Honduras	2.5	Yugoslavia	60
Iceland	1		

*The quota of Denmark shall be determined by the Fund after the Danish Government has declared its readiness to sign this Agreement but before signature takes place.

SCHEDULE B

Transitional Provisions with Respect to Repurchase, Payment of Additional Subscriptions, Gold, and Certain Operational Matters

1. Repurchase obligations that have accrued pursuant to Article V, Section 7(*b*) before the date of the second amendment of this Agreement and that remain undischarged at that date shall be discharged not later than the date or dates at which the obligations had to be discharged in accordance with the provisions of this Agreement before the second amendment.

2. A member shall discharge with special drawing rights any obligation to pay gold to the Fund in repurchase or as a subscription that is outstanding at the date of the second amendment of this Agreement, but the Fund may prescribe that these payments may be made in whole or in part in the currencies of other members specified by the Fund. A non-participant shall discharge an obligation that must be paid in special drawing rights pursuant to this provision with the currencies of other members specified by the Fund.

3. For the purposes of 2 above 0.888 671 gram of fine gold shall be equivalent to one special drawing right, and the amount of currency payable under 2 above shall be determined on that basis and on the basis of the value of the currency in terms of the special drawing right at the date of discharge.

4. A member's currency held by the Fund in excess of seventy-five percent of the member's quota at the date of the second amendment of this Agreement and not subject to repurchase under 1 above shall be repurchased in accordance with the following rules:

(i) Holdings that resulted from a purchase shall be repurchased in accordance with the policy on the use of the Fund's general resources under which the purchase was made.

(ii) Other holdings shall be repurchased not later than four years after the date of the second amendment of this Agreement.

5. Repurchases under 1 above that are not subject to 2 above, repurchases under 4 above, and any specification of currencies under 2 above shall be in accordance with Article V, Section 7(*i*).

6. All rules and regulations, rates, procedures, and decisions in effect at the date of the second amendment of this Agreement shall remain in effect until they are changed in accordance with the provisions of this Agreement.

7. To the extent that arrangements equivalent in effect to (*a*) and (*b*) below have not been completed before the date of the second amendment of this Agreement, the Fund shall

(*a*) sell up to 25 million ounces of fine gold held by it on August 31, 1975 to those members that were members on that date and that agree to buy it, in proportion to their quotas on that date. The sale to a member under this sub-paragraph (*a*) shall be made in exchange for its currency and at a price equivalent at the time of sale to one special drawing right per 0.888 671 gram of fine gold, and

(*b*) sell up to 25 million ounces of fine gold held by it on August 31, 1975 for the benefit of developing members that were members on that date, provided, however, that the part of any profits or surplus value of the gold that corresponds to the proportion of such a member's quota on August 31, 1975 to the total of the quotas of all members on that date shall be transferred directly to each such member. The requirements under Article V, Section 12(*c*) that the Fund consult a member, obtain a member's concurrence, or exchange a member's currency for the currencies of other members in certain circumstances shall apply with respect to currency received by the Fund as a result of sales of gold under this provision, other than sales to a member in return for its own currency, and placed in the General Resources Account.

Upon the sale of gold under this paragraph 7, an amount of the proceeds in the currencies received equivalent at the time of sale to one special drawing right per 0.888 671 gram of fine gold shall be placed in the General Resources Account and other assets held by the Fund under arrangements pursuant to (*b*) above shall be held separately from the general resources of the Fund. Assets that remain subject to disposition by the Fund upon termination of arrangements pursuant to (*b*) above shall be transferred to the Special Disbursement Account.

Schedule C

Par Values

1. The Fund shall notify members that par values may be established for the purposes of this Agreement, in accordance with Article IV, Sections 1, 3, 4, and 5 and this Schedule, in terms of the special drawing right, or in terms of such other common denominator as is prescribed by the Fund. The common denominator shall not be gold or a currency.

2. A member that intends to establish a par value for its currency shall propose a par value to the Fund within a reasonable time after notice is given under 1 above.

3. Any member that does not intend to establish a par value for its currency under 1 above shall consult with the Fund and ensure that its exchange arrangements are consistent with the purposes of the Fund and are adequate to fulfill its obligations under Article IV, Section 1.

4. The Fund shall concur in or object to a proposed par value within a reasonable period after receipt of the proposal. A proposed par value shall not take effect for the purposes of this Agreement if the Fund objects to it, and the member shall be subject to 3 above. The Fund shall not object because of the domestic social or political policies of the member proposing the par value.

5. Each member that has a par value for its currency undertakes to apply appropriate measures consistent with this Agreement in order to ensure that the maximum and the minimum rates for spot exchange transactions taking place within its territories between its currency and the currencies of other members maintaining par values shall not differ from parity by more than four and one-half percent or by such other margin or margins as the Fund may adopt by an eighty-five percent majority of the total voting power.

6. A member shall not propose a change in the par value of its currency except to correct, or prevent the emergence of, a fundamental disequilibrium. A change may be made only on the proposal of the member and only after consultation with the Fund.

7. When a change is proposed, the Fund shall concur in or object to the proposed par value within a reasonable period after receipt of the proposal. The Fund shall concur if it is satisfied that the change is

necessary to correct, or prevent the emergence of, a fundamental disequilibrium. The Fund shall not object because of the domestic social or political policies of the member proposing the change. A proposed change in par value shall not take effect for the purposes of this Agreement if the Fund objects to it. If a member changes the par value of its currency despite the objection of the Fund, the member shall be subject to Article XXVI, Section 2. Maintenance of an unrealistic par value by a member shall be discouraged by the Fund.

8. The par value of a member's currency established under this Agreement shall cease to exist for the purposes of this Agreement if the member informs the Fund that it intends to terminate the par value. The Fund may object to the termination of a par value by a decision taken by an eighty-five percent majority of the total voting power. If a member terminates a par value for its currency despite the objection of the Fund, the member shall be subject to Article XXVI, Section 2. A par value established under this Agreement shall cease to exist for the purposes of this Agreement if the member terminates the par value despite the objection of the Fund, or if the Fund finds that the member does not maintain rates for a substantial volume of exchange transactions in accordance with 5 above, provided that the Fund may not make such finding unless it has consulted the member and given it sixty days notice of the Fund's intention to consider whether to make a finding.

9. If the par value of the currency of a member has ceased to exist under 8 above, the member shall consult with the Fund and ensure that its exchange arrangements are consistent with the purposes of the Fund and are adequate to fulfill its obligations under Article IV, Section 1.

10. A member for whose currency the par value has ceased to exist under 8 above may, at any time, propose a new par value for its currency.

11. Notwithstanding 6 above, the Fund, by a seventy percent majority of the total voting power, may make uniform proportionate changes in all par values if the special drawing right is the common denominator and the changes will not affect the value of the special drawing right. The par value of a member's currency shall, however, not be changed under this provision if, within seven days after the Fund's action, the member informs the Fund that it does not wish the par value of its currency to be changed by such action.

SCHEDULE D

Council

1. (*a*) Each member that appoints an Executive Director and each group of members that has the number of votes allotted to them cast by an elected Executive Director shall appoint to the Council one Councillor, who shall be a Governor, Minister in the government of a member, or person of comparable rank, and may appoint not more than seven Associates. The Board of Governors may change, by an eighty-five percent majority of the total voting power, the number of Associates who may be appointed. A Councillor or Associate shall serve until a new appointment is made or until the next regular election of Executive Directors, whichever shall occur sooner.

(*b*) Executive Directors, or in their absence their Alternates, and Associates shall be entitled to attend meetings of the Council, unless the Council decides to hold a restricted session. Each member and each group of members that appoints a Councillor shall appoint an Alternate who shall be entitled to attend a meeting of the Council when the Councillor is not present, and shall have full power to act for the Councillor.

2. (*a*) The Council shall supervise the management and adaptation of the international monetary system, including the continuing operation of the adjustment process and developments in global liquidity, and in this connection shall review developments in the transfer of real resources to developing countries.

(*b*) The Council shall consider proposals pursuant to Article XXVIII(*a*) to amend the Articles of Agreement.

3. (*a*) The Board of Governors may delegate to the Council authority to exercise any powers of the Board of Governors except the powers conferred directly by this Agreement on the Board of Governors.

(*b*) Each Councillor shall be entitled to cast the number of votes allotted under Article XII, Section 5 to the member or group of members appointing him. A Councillor appointed by a group of members may cast separately the votes allotted to each member in the group. If the number of votes allotted to a member cannot be cast by an Executive Director, the member may make arrangements with a Councillor for casting the number of votes allotted to the member.

(*c*) The Council shall not take any action pursuant to powers delegated by the Board of Governors that is inconsistent with any action taken by the Board of Governors and the Executive Board shall not take any action pursuant to powers delegated by the Board of Governors that is inconsistent with any action taken by either the Board of Governors or the Council.

4. The Council shall select a Councillor as chairman, shall adopt regulations as may be necessary or appropriate to perform its functions, and shall determine any aspect of its procedure. The Council shall hold such meetings as may be provided for by the Council or called by the Executive Board.

5. (*a*) The Council shall have powers corresponding to those of the Executive Board under the following provisions: Article XII, Section 2(*c*), (*f*), (*g*), and (*j*); Article XVIII, Section 4(*a*) and Section 4(*c*)(iv); Article XXIII, Section 1; and Article XXVII, Section 1(*a*).

(*b*) For decisions by the Council on matters pertaining exclusively to the Special Drawing Rights Department only Councillors appointed by a member that is a participant or a group of members at least one member of which is a participant shall be entitled to vote. Each of these Councillors shall be entitled to cast the number of votes allotted to the member which is a participant that appointed him or to the members that are participants in the group of members that appointed him, and may cast the votes allotted to a participant with which arrangements have been made pursuant to the last sentence of 3(*b*) above.

(*c*) The Council may by regulation establish a procedure whereby the Executive Board may obtain a vote of the Councillors on a specific question without a meeting of the Council when in the judgment of the Executive Board an action must be taken by the Council which should not be postponed until the next meeting of the Council and which does not warrant the calling of a special meeting.

(*d*) Article IX, Section 8 shall apply to Councillors, their Alternates, and Associates, and to any other person entitled to attend a meeting of the Council.

(*e*) For the purposes of (*b*) and 3(*b*) above, an agreement under Article XII, Section 3(*i*)(ii) by a member, or by a member that is a participant, shall entitle a Councillor to vote and cast the number of votes allotted to the member.

(*f*) When an Executive Director is entitled to cast the number of votes allotted to a member pursuant to Article XII, Section 3(*i*)(v), the Councillor appointed by the group whose members elected such Executive Director shall be entitled to vote and cast the number of votes allotted to such member. The member shall be deemed to have participated in the appointment of the Councillor entitled to vote and cast the number of votes allotted to the member.

6. The first sentence of Article XII, Section 2(*a*) shall be deemed to include a reference to the Council.

Schedule E

Election of Executive Directors

1. The election of the elective Executive Directors shall be by ballot of the Governors eligible to vote.

2. In balloting for the Executive Directors to be elected, each of the Governors eligible to vote shall cast for one person all of the votes to which he is entitled under Article XII, Section 5(*a*). The fifteen persons receiving the greatest number of votes shall be Executive Directors, provided that no person who received less than four percent of the total number of votes that can be cast (eligible votes) shall be considered elected.

3. When fifteen persons are not elected in the first ballot, a second ballot shall be held in which there shall vote only (*a*) those Governors who voted in the first ballot for a person not elected, and (*b*) those Governors whose votes for a person elected are deemed under 4 below to have raised the votes cast for that person above nine percent of the eligible votes. If in the second ballot there are more candidates than the number of Executive Directors to be elected, the person

who received the lowest number of votes in the first ballot shall be ineligible for election.

4. In determining whether the votes cast by a Governor are to be deemed to have raised the total of any person above nine percent of the eligible votes the nine percent shall be deemed to include, first, the votes of the Governor casting the largest number of votes for such person, then the votes of the Governor casting the next largest number, and so on until nine percent is reached.

5. Any Governor part of whose votes must be counted in order to raise the total of any person above four percent shall be considered as casting all of his votes for such person even if the total votes for such person thereby exceed nine percent.

6. If, after the second ballot, fifteen persons have not been elected, further ballots shall be held on the same principles until fifteen persons have been elected, provided that after fourteen persons are elected, the fifteenth may be elected by a simple majority of the remaining votes and shall be deemed to have been elected by all such votes.

SCHEDULE F

Designation

During the first basic period the rules for designation shall be as follows:

(*a*) Participants subject to designation under Article XIX, Section 5(*a*)(i) shall be designated for such amounts as will promote over time equality in the ratios of the participants' holdings of special drawing rights in excess of their net cumulative allocations to their official holdings of gold and foreign exchange.

(*b*) The formula to give effect to (*a*) above shall be such that participants subject to designation shall be designated:

(i) in proportion to their official holdings of gold and foreign exchange when the ratios described in (*a*) above are equal; and

(ii) in such manner as gradually to reduce the difference between the ratios described in (*a*) above that are low and the ratios that are high.

SCHEDULE G

Reconstitution

1. During the first basic period the rules for reconstitution shall be as follows:

(*a*) (i) A participant shall so use and reconstitute its holdings of special drawing rights that, five years after the first allocation and at the end of each calendar quarter thereafter, the average of its total daily holdings of special drawing rights over the most recent five-year period will be not less than thirty percent of the average of its daily net cumulative allocation of special drawing rights over the same period.

(ii) Two years after the first allocation and at the end of each calendar month thereafter the Fund shall make calculations for each participant so as to ascertain whether and to what extent the participant would need to acquire special drawing rights between the date of the calculation and the end of any five-year period in order to comply with the requirement in (*a*)(i) above. The Fund shall adopt regulations with respect to the bases on which these calculations shall be made and with respect to the timing of the designation of participants under Article XIX, Section 5(*a*)(ii), in order to assist them to comply with the requirement in (*a*)(i) above.

(iii) The Fund shall give special notice to a participant when the calculations under (*a*)(ii) above indicate that it is unlikely that the participant will be able to comply with the requirement in (*a*)(i) above unless it ceases to use special drawing rights for the rest of the period for which the calculation was made under (*a*)(ii) above.

(iv) A participant that needs to acquire special drawing rights to fulfill this obligation shall be obligated and entitled to obtain them, for currency acceptable to the Fund, in a transaction with the Fund conducted through the General Resources Account. If sufficient special drawing rights to fulfill this obligation cannot be obtained in this way, the participant shall be obligated and entitled to obtain them with a freely usable currency from a participant which the Fund shall specify.

(*b*) Participants shall also pay due regard to the desirability of pursuing over time a balanced relationship between their holdings of special drawing rights and their other reserves.

2. If a participant fails to comply with the rules for reconstitution, the Fund shall determine whether or not the circumstances justify suspension under Article XXIII, Section 2(*b*).

Schedule H

Termination of Participation

1. If the obligation remaining after the setoff under Article XXIV, Section 2(*b*) is to the terminating participant and agreement on settlement between the Fund and the terminating participant is not reached within six months of the date of termination, the Fund shall redeem this balance of special drawing rights in equal half-yearly installments within a maximum of five years of the date of termination. The Fund shall redeem this balance as it may determine, either (*a*) by the payment to the terminating participant of the amounts provided by the remaining participants to the Fund in accordance with Article XXIV, Section 5, or (*b*) by permitting the terminating participant to use its special drawing rights to obtain its own currency or a freely usable currency from a participant specified by the Fund, the General Resources Account, or any other holder.

2. If the obligation remaining after the setoff under Article XXIV, Section 2(*b*) is to the Fund and agreement on settlement is not reached within six months of the date of termination, the terminating participant shall discharge this obligation in equal half-yearly installments within three years of the date of termination or within such longer period as may be fixed by the Fund. The terminating participant shall discharge this obligation, as the Fund may determine, either (*a*) by the payment to the Fund of a freely usable currency, or (*b*) by obtaining special drawing rights, in accordance with Article XXIV, Section 6, from the General Resources Account or in agreement with a participant specified by the Fund or from any other holder, and the setoff of these special drawing rights against the installment due.

3. Installments under either 1 or 2 above shall fall due six months after the date of termination and at intervals of six months thereafter.

4. In the event of the Special Drawing Rights Department going into liquidation under Article XXV within six months of the date a

participant terminates its participation, the settlement between the Fund and that government shall be made in accordance with Article XXV and Schedule I.

Schedule I

Administration of Liquidation of the Special Drawing Rights Department

1. In the event of liquidation of the Special Drawing Rights Department, participants shall discharge their obligations to the Fund in ten half-yearly installments, or in such longer period as the Fund may decide is needed, in a freely usable currency and the currencies of participants holding special drawing rights to be redeemed in any installment to the extent of such redemption, as determined by the Fund. The first half-yearly payment shall be made six months after the decision to liquidate the Special Drawing Rights Department.

2. If it is decided to liquidate the Fund within six months of the date of the decision to liquidate the Special Drawing Rights Department, the liquidation of the Special Drawing Rights Department shall not proceed until special drawing rights held in the General Resources Account have been distributed in accordance with the following rule:

> After the distributions made under 2(*a*) and (*b*) of Schedule K, the Fund shall apportion its special drawing rights held in the General Resources Account among all members that are participants in proportion to the amounts due to each participant after the distribution under 2(*b*). To determine the amount due to each member for the purpose of apportioning the remainder of its holdings of each currency under 2(*d*) of Schedule K, the Fund shall deduct the distribution of special drawing rights made under this rule.

3. With the amounts received under 1 above, the Fund shall redeem special drawing rights held by holders in the following manner and order:

(*a*) Special drawing rights held by governments that have terminated their participation more than six months before the date the Board of Governors decides to liquidate the Special Drawing Rights Department shall be redeemed in accordance with the terms of any agreement under Article XXIV or Schedule H.

(*b*) Special drawing rights held by holders that are not participants shall be redeemed before those held by participants, and shall be redeemed in proportion to the amount held by each holder.

(*c*) The Fund shall determine the proportion of special drawing rights held by each participant in relation to its net cumulative allocation. The Fund shall first redeem special drawing rights from the participants with the highest proportion until this proportion is reduced to that of the second highest proportion; the Fund shall then redeem the special drawing rights held by these participants in accordance with their net cumulative allocations until the proportions are reduced to that of the third highest proportion; and this process shall be continued until the amount available for redemption is exhausted.

4. Any amount that a participant will be entitled to receive in redemption under 3 above shall be set off against any amount to be paid under 1 above.

5. During liquidation the Fund shall pay interest on the amount of special drawing rights held by holders, and each participant shall pay charges on the net cumulative allocation of special drawing rights to it less the amount of any payments made in accordance with 1 above. The rates of interest and charges and the time of payment shall be determined by the Fund. Payments of interest and charges shall be made in special drawing rights to the extent possible. A participant that does not hold sufficient special drawing rights to meet any charges shall make the payment with a currency specified by the Fund. Special drawing rights received as charges in amounts needed for administrative expenses shall not be used for the payment of interest, but shall be transferred to the Fund and shall be redeemed first and with the currencies used by the Fund to meet its expenses.

6. While a participant is in default with respect to any payment required by 1 or 5 above, no amounts shall be paid to it in accordance with 3 or 5 above.

7. If after the final payments have been made to participants each participant not in default does not hold special drawing rights in the same proportion to its net cumulative allocation, those participants holding a lower proportion shall purchase from those holding a higher proportion such amounts in accordance with arrangements made by the Fund as will make the proportion of their holdings of

special drawing rights the same. Each participant in default shall pay to the Fund its own currency in an amount equal to its default. The Fund shall apportion this currency and residual claims among participants in proportion to the amount of special drawing rights held by each and these special drawing rights shall be cancelled. The Fund shall then close the books of the Special Drawing Rights Department and all of the Fund's liabilities arising from the allocations of special drawing rights and the administration of the Special Drawing Rights Department shall cease.

8. Each participant whose currency is distributed to other participants under this Schedule guarantees the unrestricted use of such currency at all times for the purchase of goods or for payments of sums due to it or to persons in its territories. Each participant so obligated agrees to compensate other participants for any loss resulting from the difference between the value at which the Fund distributed its currency under this Schedule and the value realized by such participants on disposal of its currency.

Schedule J

Settlement of Accounts with Members Withdrawing

1. The settlement of accounts with respect to the General Resources Account shall be made according to 1 to 6 of this Schedule. The Fund shall be obligated to pay to a member withdrawing an amount equal to its quota, plus any other amounts due to it from the Fund, less any amounts due to the Fund, including charges accruing after the date of its withdrawal; but no payment shall be made until six months after the date of withdrawal. Payments shall be made in the currency of the withdrawing member, and for this purpose the Fund may transfer to the General Resources Account holdings of the member's currency in the Special Disbursement Account or in the Investment Account in exchange for an equivalent amount of the currencies of other members in the General Resources Account selected by the Fund with their concurrence.

2. If the Fund's holdings of the currency of the withdrawing member are not sufficient to pay the net amount due from the Fund, the balance shall be paid in a freely usable currency, or in such other manner as may be agreed. If the Fund and the withdrawing member do not reach agreement within six months of the date of withdrawal, the currency in question held by the Fund shall be paid forthwith to the withdrawing member. Any balance due shall be paid in ten half-

yearly installments during the ensuing five years. Each such installment shall be paid, at the option of the Fund, either in the currency of the withdrawing member acquired after its withdrawal or in a freely usable currency.

3. If the Fund fails to meet any installment which is due in accordance with the preceding paragraphs, the withdrawing member shall be entitled to require the Fund to pay the installment in any currency held by the Fund with the exception of any currency which has been declared scarce under Article VII, Section 3.

4. If the Fund's holdings of the currency of a withdrawing member exceed the amount due to it, and if agreement on the method of settling accounts is not reached within six months of the date of withdrawal, the former member shall be obligated to redeem such excess currency in a freely usable currency. Redemption shall be made at the rates at which the Fund would sell such currencies at the time of withdrawal from the Fund. The withdrawing member shall complete redemption within five years of the date of withdrawal, or within such longer period as may be fixed by the Fund, but shall not be required to redeem in any half-yearly period more than one-tenth of the Fund's excess holdings of its currency at the date of withdrawal plus further acquisitions of the currency during such half-yearly period. If the withdrawing member does not fulfill this obligation, the Fund may in an orderly manner liquidate in any market the amount of currency which should have been redeemed.

5. Any member desiring to obtain the currency of a member which has withdrawn shall acquire it by purchase from the Fund, to the extent that such member has access to the general resources of the Fund and that such currency is available under 4 above.

6. The withdrawing member guarantees the unrestricted use at all times of the currency disposed of under 4 and 5 above for the purchase of goods or for payment of sums due to it or to persons within its territories. It shall compensate the Fund for any loss resulting from the difference between the value of its currency in terms of the special drawing right on the date of withdrawal and the value realized in terms of the special drawing right by the Fund on disposal under 4 and 5 above.

7. If the withdrawing member is indebted to the Fund as the result of transactions conducted through the Special Disbursement Account under Article V, Section 12(*f*)(ii), the indebtedness shall be discharged in accordance with the terms of the indebtedness.

8. If the Fund holds the withdrawing member's currency in the Special Disbursement Account or in the Investment Account, the Fund may in an orderly manner exchange in any market for the currencies of members the amount of the currency of the withdrawing member remaining in each account after use under 1 above, and the proceeds of the exchange of the amount in each account shall be kept in that account. Paragraph 5 above and the first sentence of 6 above shall apply to the withdrawing member's currency.

9. If the Fund holds obligations of the withdrawing member in the Special Disbursement Account pursuant to Article V, Section 12(*h*), or in the Investment Account, the Fund may hold them until the date of maturity or dispose of them sooner. Paragraph 8 above shall apply to the proceeds of such disinvestment.

10. In the event of the Fund going into liquidation under Article XXVII, Section 2 within six months of the date on which the member withdraws, the accounts between the Fund and that government shall be settled in accordance with Article XXVII, Section 2 and Schedule K.

Schedule K

Administration of Liquidation

1. In the event of liquidation the liabilities of the Fund other than the repayment of subscriptions shall have priority in the distribution of the assets of the Fund. In meeting each such liability the Fund shall use its assets in the following order:

(*a*) the currency in which the liability is payable;

(*b*) gold;

(*c*) all other currencies in proportion, so far as may be practicable, to the quotas of the members.

2. After the discharge of the Fund's liabilities in accordance with 1 above, the balance of the Fund's assets shall be distributed and apportioned as follows:

(*a*) (i) The Fund shall calculate the value of gold held on August 31, 1975 that it continues to hold on the date of the decision to liquidate. The calculation shall be made in accordance with 9 below and also on the basis of one special drawing right per 0.888 671 gram of fine gold on the date of liquidation. Gold equivalent to the excess of the former value over the latter shall be distributed to those members that were members on August 31, 1975 in proportion to their quotas on that date.

(ii) The Fund shall distribute any assets held in the Special Disbursement Account on the date of the decision to liquidate to those members that were members on August 31, 1975 in proportion to their quotas on that date. Each type of asset shall be distributed proportionately to members.

(*b*) The Fund shall distribute its remaining holdings of gold among the members whose currencies are held by the Fund in amounts less than their quotas in the proportions, but not in excess of, the amounts by which their quotas exceed the Fund's holdings of their currencies.

(*c*) The Fund shall distribute to each member one-half the Fund's holdings of its currency but such distribution shall not exceed fifty percent of its quota.

(*d*) The Fund shall apportion the remainder of its holdings of gold and each currency

(i) among all members in proportion to, but not in excess of, the amounts due to each member after the distributions under (*b*) and (*c*) above, provided that distribution under 2(*a*) above shall not be taken into account for determining the amounts due, and

(ii) any excess holdings of gold and currency among all the members in proportion to their quotas.

3. Each member shall redeem the holdings of its currency apportioned to other members under 2(*d*) above, and shall agree with the Fund within three months after a decision to liquidate upon an orderly procedure for such redemption.

4. If a member has not reached agreement with the Fund within the three-month period referred to in 3 above, the Fund shall use the currencies of other members apportioned to that member under 2(*d*) above to redeem the currency of that member apportioned to other members. Each currency apportioned to a member which has not reached agreement shall be used, so far as possible, to redeem its

currency apportioned to the members which have made agreements with the Fund under 3 above.

5. If a member has reached agreement with the Fund in accordance with 3 above, the Fund shall use the currencies of other members apportioned to that member under 2(*d*) above to redeem the currency of that member apportioned to other members which have made agreements with the Fund under 3 above. Each amount so redeemed shall be redeemed in the currency of the member to which it was apportioned.

6. After carrying out the steps in the preceding paragraphs, the Fund shall pay to each member the remaining currencies held for its account.

7. Each member whose currency has been distributed to other members under 6 above shall redeem such currency in the currency of the member requesting redemption, or in such other manner as may be agreed between them. If the members involved do not otherwise agree, the member obligated to redeem shall complete redemption within five years of the date of distribution, but shall not be required to redeem in any half-yearly period more than one-tenth of the amount distributed to each other member. If the member does not fulfill this obligation, the amount of currency which should have been redeemed may be liquidated in an orderly manner in any market.

8. Each member whose currency has been distributed to other members under 6 above guarantees the unrestricted use of such currency at all times for the purchase of goods or for payment of sums due to it or to persons in its territories. Each member so obligated agrees to compensate other members for any loss resulting from the difference between the value of its currency in terms of the special drawing right on the date of the decision to liquidate the Fund and the value in terms of the special drawing right realized by such members on disposal of its currency.

9. The Fund shall determine the value of gold under this Schedule on the basis of prices in the market.

10. For the purposes of this Schedule, quotas shall be deemed to have been increased to the full extent to which they could have been increased in accordance with Article III, Section 2(*b*) of this Agreement.

Schedule L

Suspension of Voting Rights

In the case of a suspension of voting rights of a member under Article XXVI, Section 2(*b*), the following provisions shall apply:

1. The member shall not:

(*a*) participate in the adoption of a proposed amendment of this Agreement, or be counted in the total number of members for that purpose, except in the case of an amendment requiring acceptance by all members under Article XXVIII(*b*) or pertaining exclusively to the Special Drawing Rights Department;

(*b*) appoint a Governor or Alternate Governor, appoint or participate in the appointment of a Councillor or Alternate Councillor, or appoint, elect, or participate in the election of an Executive Director.

2. The number of votes allotted to the member shall not be cast in any organ of the Fund. They shall not be included in the calculation of the total voting power, except for purposes of the acceptance of a proposed amendment pertaining exclusively to the Special Drawing Rights Department.

3. (*a*) The Governor and Alternate Governor appointed by the member shall cease to hold office.

(*b*) The Councillor and Alternate Councillor appointed by the member, or in whose appointment the member has participated, shall cease to hold office, provided that, if such Councillor was entitled to cast the number of votes allotted to other members whose voting rights have not been suspended, another Councillor and Alternate Councillor shall be appointed by such other members under Schedule D, and, pending such appointment, the Councillor and Alternate Councillor shall continue to hold office, but for a maximum of thirty days from the date of suspension.

(*c*) The Executive Director appointed or elected by the member, or in whose election the member has participated, shall cease to hold office, unless such Executive Director was entitled to cast the number of votes allotted to other members whose voting rights have not been suspended. In the latter case:

(i) if more than ninety days remain before the next regular election of Executive Directors, another Executive Director shall be elected for the remainder of the term by such other members by a majority of the votes cast; pending such election, the Executive Director shall continue to hold office, but for a maximum of thirty days from the date of suspension;

(ii) if not more than ninety days remain before the next regular election of Executive Directors, the Executive Director shall continue to hold office for the remainder of the term.

4. The member shall be entitled to send a representative to attend any meeting of the Board of Governors, the Council, or the Executive Board, but not any meeting of their committees, when a request made by, or a matter particularly affecting, the member is under consideration.

INDEX

Index

Executive Directors *(continued)*
Alternate, determination of remuneration by Board of Governors, Art. XII, Sec. 2(*i*)
Alternate, entitlement to attend meetings of Council, Sched. D, par. 1(*b*)
Alternate, immunities and privileges, Art. IX, Sec. 8, 9(*b*)
Appointed, Art. XII, Sec. 3(*b*)(i), 3(*c*), 3(*i*)
Attendance at Council meetings, Sched. D, par. 1(*b*)
Cessation of office after suspension of voting rights, Sched. L, par. 3(*c*)
Election, Art. XII, Sec. 3(*b*)(ii), (*d*); Sched. E
Elective, Art. XII, Sec. 3(*b*)(ii)
Immunities and privileges, Art. IX, Sec. 8
Immunity from tax on salaries, Art. IX, Sec. 9(*b*)
Increase or decrease in number to be elected, Art. XII, Sec. 3(*b*)
Number, Art. XII, Sec. 3(*b*), (*c*)
Remuneration, determination by Board of Governors, Art. XII, Sec. 2(*i*)
Suspension of member's right to appoint or participate in election, Sched. L, par. 1(*b*)
Vacancy in office of elected Executive Director, Art. XII, Sec. 3(*f*)
Votes, number for each Executive Director, Art. XII, Sec. 3(*i*), 5
Explanation of terms, Art. XXX (*see also* Definition of terms)

Financial and technical services, performance by Fund, Art. V, Sec. 2(*b*)
Fiscal agencies:
Dealing with Fund, Art. V, Sec. 1
Not to engage in discriminatory currency arrangements or multiple currency practices, Art. VIII, Sec. 3
Undertakings with respect to transactions with non-member, Art. XI, Sec. 1(i); Art. XXVII, Sec. 1(*a*)(iii)
Foreign exchange, data members may be required to furnish, Art. VIII, Sec. 5(*a*)(i), (ii)
Freely usable currency:
Conversion into by member whose currency has been purchased from Fund, Art. V, Sec. 3(*e*)
Definition, Art. XXX(*f*)
Exchange for currency specified for repurchase, Art. V, Sec. 7(*i*)
Obligation to provide on demand to participant using special drawing rights, Art. XIX, Sec. 4
Settlement with members withdrawing, Sched. J, par. 2, 4
Settlement with terminating participant, Art. XXIV, Sec. 5, 6; Sched. H
Use to acquire special drawing rights for payment of charge or assessment, Art. XX, Sec. 5; Art. XXIV, Sec. 3
Use to discharge obligations to Fund by participants in event of liquidation of Special Drawing Rights Department, Sched. I, par. 1
Use to obtain special drawing rights to fulfill reconstitution obligation, Sched. G, par. 1(*a*)(iv)
Fundamental disequilibrium; *see* Disequilibrium

Special Drawing Rights Department *(continued)*
Establishment and operation, Introd. Art. (ii), (iii)
Expenses of conducting business, reimbursement to General Department, Art. XVI, Sec. 2; Art. XX, Sec. 4, 5
General obligations of participants, Art. XXII
Indication of decisions relating to, Art. XXI(*a*)(iii)
Interest and charges, Art. XX; Art. XXIV, Sec. 3
Liquidation, Art. XXV; Sched. I
Non-participants' payments when quotas are changed, Art. III, Sec. 3(*a*)
Operations and transactions, Introd. Art. (ii), (iii); Art. XVI, Sec. 1; Art. XVII, Sec. 2
Right of members to participate, Introd. Art. (ii)
Separation from General Department, Introd. Art. (ii), (iii); Art. XVI, Sec. 1, 2
Temporary suspension of operations in event of emergency or unforeseen circumstances, Art. XXIII, Sec. 1
Termination of participation, Art. XXIV; Sched. H
Special reserve; *see* Reserves of Fund
Spot exchange transactions, Art. XXVII, Sec. 1(*a*)(iv); Sched. C, par. 5
Stability; *see* Exchange stability
Stabilization fund, agency dealing with Fund, Art. V, Sec. 1
Staff:
Appointment and organization, Art. XII, Sec. 4(*b*), (*d*)
Duty to Fund, Art. XII, Sec. 4(*c*)
Immunities and privileges, Art. IX, Sec. 8, 9(*b*)
Managing Director to be chief of operating staff, Art. XII, Sec. 4(*b*)
Provision for, Art. XII, Sec. 1
Stand-by arrangements:
Charge, Art. V, Sec. 8(*a*)(ii)
Definition, Art. XXX(*b*)
Policies, adoption, Art. V, Sec. 3(*a*)
Status, immunities, and privileges:
Accorded to Fund in territories of each member, Art. IX, Sec. 1
Action by each member in its own territory, Art. IX, Sec. 10
Freedom of assets from restrictions, Art. IX, Sec. 6
Immunities and privileges of officers and employees, Art. IX, Sec. 8; Sched. D, par. 5(*d*)
Immunities from taxation, Art. IX, Sec. 9; Art. XXI(*b*)
Immunity from judicial process, Art. IX, Sec. 3
Immunity from other action, Art. IX, Sec. 4
Immunity of archives, Art. IX, Sec. 5
Juridical personality of Fund, Art. IX, Sec. 2
Privilege for communications, Art. IX, Sec. 7
Status of Fund, Art. IX, Sec. 2
Subscriptions:
Amount to be transmitted to U.S. Government when the Agreement is signed, Art. XXXI, Sec. 2(*d*), (*h*)

Treasury, agency dealing with Fund, Art. V, Sec. 1

Unexpected major developments, change in rates or intervals for allocation or cancellation of special drawing rights, Art. XVIII, Sec. 3, 4(*a*), (*d*)
Unforeseen circumstances, Art. XXIII, Sec. 1; Art. XXVII, Sec. 1(*a*); Sched. D, par. 5(*a*)
United States Government:
Deposit of instrument of acceptance with, Art. XXXI, Sec. 2(*a*)
Obligation to inform all members of signatures to the Agreement and deposit of instruments of acceptance, Art. XXXI, Sec. 2(*c*)
Partial payment of subscription transmitted to, for administrative expenses, Art. XXXI, Sec. 2(*d*), (*h*)
Use of Fund's general resources (*see also* Operations and transactions):
Buffer stocks, international, financing of contributions to, Art. XXX(*c*)(ii)
Capital transfers, Art. VI, Sec. 1, 2; Art. XXVI, Sec. 2(*a*); Art. XXVII, Sec. 1(*a*)(ii)
Charges, Art. V, Sec. 8; Art. XXVII, Sec. 1(*a*)(i)
Compensatory financing of export fluctuations, Art. XXX(*c*)(i)
Conditions governing use, Art. V, Sec. 3; Art. XXVII, Sec. 1(*a*)(i)
Currencies to be used in repurchases, policies and procedures, Art. V, Sec. 7(*i*)
Ineligibility, change in par value despite Fund objection, Sched. C, par. 7
Ineligibility, distribution of proceeds of gold sales to developing members when ineligibility ceases, Art. V, Sec. 12(*e*), (*f*)(iii)
Ineligibility, exception to obligation to buy foreign-held balances of currency, Art. VIII, Sec. 4(*b*)(v)
Ineligibility, failure to fulfill obligations, Art. V, Sec. 5; Art. VI, Sec. 1(*a*); Art. XXIII, Sec. 2(*f*); Art. XXVI, Sec. 2(*a*)
Ineligibility if member persists in maintaining restrictions, Art. XIV, Sec. 3
Ineligibility, not previously declared by Fund, Art. V, Sec. 3(*b*)(iv)
Ineligibility, termination of par value despite Fund objection, Sched. C, par. 8
Limitation because of use of resources contrary to Fund's purposes, Art. V, Sec. 5
Policies, Art. V, Sec. 3(*a*), (*c*), (*d*)
Proceeds of sale of gold, Art. V, Sec. 12(*f*)
Purchase of currency of member which has withdrawn, Sched. J, par. 5
Request for purchase, examination, Art. V, Sec. 3(*c*)
Requirement of need, Art. V, Sec. 3(*b*)(ii)
Reserve tranche purchase, Art. V, Sec. 3(*b*)(iii), (*c*); Art. XXX(*c*)
Selection of currencies to be sold, Art. V, Sec. 3(*d*)
Special policies for special balance of payments problems, Art. V, Sec. 3(*a*), 7(*d*), (*f*)
Stand-by or similar arrangements, Art. V, Sec. 3(*a*), 8(*a*)(ii); Art. XXX(*b*)
Temporary suspension, Art. XXVII, Sec. 1
Temporary use under adequate safeguards, Art. I(v); Art. V, Sec. 3(*a*)
Waiver of conditions, Art. V, Sec. 4

International Monetary Fund, Washington D.C. 20431, U.S.A.
Telephone number: 202 623 7000
Cable address: Interfund